GENERAL EDITOR DAVID G. CHANDLER

OSPREY MILITARY · **CAMPAIGN SERIES** · 4

TET OFFENSIVE 1968

TURNING POINT IN VIETNAM

JAMES R. ARNOLD

First published in 1990 by Osprey Publishing Ltd, 59 Grosvenor Street, London W1X 9DA.

British Library Cataloguing in Publication Data
Arnold, James R. 1952–
Tet offensive, 1968: the turning point in Vietnam
1. Vietnamese Wars, 1961–1975
I. Title
959.704'3
ISBN 0-85045-960-5

Produced by DAG Publications Ltd for Osprey Publishing Ltd.
Colour bird's eye view illustrations by Cilla Eurich.
Cartography by Micromap.
Wargaming Tet by Alan Hamilton.
Wargames consultant Duncan Macfarlane.
Typeset by Typesetters (Birmingham) Ltd, Warley, West Midlands.
Mono camerawork by M&E Reproductions, North Fambridge, Essex.
Printed and bound in Hong Kong.

The photographs reproduced in this volume were provided by the US Department of Defense Still Media Records Centre, Washington, DC.

Key to Map Symbols

Army Group	XXXXX ⊠	Infantry	⊠
Army	XXXX ⊠	Cavalry	◥
Corps	XXX ⊠	Artillery	•
Division	XX ⊠	Armour	⬭
Brigade	X ⊠	Motorized	⊗
Regiment	III ⊠	Airborne	⊠
Battalion	II ⊠	Special Forces	⊠

Acknowledgements

Numerous people contributed to the completion of this book. My wife, Roberta Wiener, edited the manuscript and served as picture researcher, helping to locate and select the photographs. John Moore, of Military Archive and Research Services in Braceborough, England, taught Roberta and me how to conduct photo research. Steve Everett of the Center for Military History, Washington, DC, provided transcripts of interviews with Vietnam veterans from his Oral History Archives. Dorothy McConchie and Robert Waller of the US Department of Defense Still Media Records Center in Washington, DC, were most helpful in guiding us through their tremendous photograph collection. The reference librarians, most especially Ben Ritter, at Handley Library in Winchester, Virginia, cheerfully and quickly processed my long list of inter-library loan requests. I wish to thank you all.

OSPREY
MILITARY

CAMPAIGN SERIES   4

TET OFFENSIVE 1968

The M-60 machine-gun was a belt-fed, gas-operated, air-cooled weapon that fired a 7.62mm round to an effective range of 1,100 yards. It had a sustained rate of fire of some 100 rounds per minute. Without mount or ammunition, it weighed 23 pounds and was thus carried on jungle patrol.

CONTENTS

BACKGROUND TO SURPRISE

The supreme command for the Viet Cong/North Vietnamese Army (VC/NVA) forces had a coherent strategy for conquering South Vietnam that the Americans neither fully appreciated nor effectively countered. In general terms, Communist strategists followed Mao Tse-tung's principles of guerrilla war. But ever inventive, the Vietnamese Communists adapted strategies for their unique circumstances. It was a strategy devised in the early 1960s when America only had advisers in Vietnam, and tenaciously clung to during the difficult years of massive US military activity until final victory. In essence it proved a war-winning strategy.

The overriding goal was to effect a withdrawal of American forces from South Vietnam to bring about negotiations leading to a new, Communist-dominated government in the south. To achieve this political end, the National Liberation Front fought on three fronts: political, military and diplomatic. The political battle involved mobilizing support from the people of South Vietnam while undermining the South Vietnamese government. The military component required confronting the Americans and their allies on the battlefield to inflict losses whenever possible. On the battlefield there were no objectives that had to be held. The diplomatic element of the three-prong strategy focused on mobilizing international opposition to the American war effort and promoting anti-war sentiment in the United States. As explained by a high-ranking Viet Cong:

'Every military clash, every demonstration, every propaganda appeal was seen as part of an integrated whole; each had consequences far beyond its immediately apparent results. It was a framework that allowed us to view battles as psychological events.'

In mid-1967, the Communist high command decided that the time was ripe for the crowning psychological event, a surprise nation-wide offensive to coincide with the Tet holidays.

About the time when Communist planning for the Tet Offensive began, top-level American civilian and military planners met in Honolulu. The conference focused on how to interdict the flow of enemy troops and material into South Vietnam. Inevitably, this led to consideration of higher strategy. The conference's final report stated: 'A clear concise statement of US strategy in Vietnam could not be established . . . A war of attrition provides neither economy of force nor any foreseeable end to the war.' The conference could simply not identify anything worthy of being called a strategy.

In the broadest terms, the American high command had pursued a two-part scheme since 1966. General William C. Westmoreland described this approach in an interview as the Tet Offensive was winding down: '. . . the [South] Vietnamese forces would concentrate on providing security to the populated areas, while the US forces would provide a shield behind which pacification could be carried out'. The idea was that the American forces would operate away from populated areas where they could use their superior firepower and mobility to counter the North Vietnamese Army and Viet Cong mainforce units. Speaking after the war, Marine Corps historian and Vietnam veteran Brigadier General Edwin Simmons commented:

'It's true we violated many of the basic principles of war. We had no clear objective. We had no unity of command. We never had the initiative. The most common phrase was "reaction force" – we were reacting to them. Our forces were divided and diffused. Since we didn't have a clear objective, we had to measure our performance by statistics.'

Thus the sterile tabulation of 'Battalion Days in

According to Westmoreland's strategy, US forces were to engage regular enemy formations while ARVN forces concentrated on pacification. The problem was finding the enemy. Men of the 1st Cavalry Division (Airmobile) – the élite 'First Team' – conduct combat assault into the An Lao Valley.

During the months leading up to the Tet Offensive, President Lyndon Johnson and his administration told the American public that the Allies were winning the war. This left the public unbraced for the coming shock. A well-intentioned man, Johnson lacked the vision to guide the country to a satisfactory resolution of the war. Here he shakes hands during a visit to a hospital at Cam Ranh Bay in 1967.

the Field', hamlets 'controlled', or most notably 'body count' replaced clear strategic direction.

President Lyndon Johnson tried to counter the growing public doubts about the war by a carefully crafted propaganda campaign in late 1967. It claimed that the Communists were slowly losing the war. He sought to gain support for a long-term, limited-war policy. With hindsight it is clear that this approach contained neither a decisive war-winning stategy nor a plausible diplomatic outcome. Worse, from the administration's stand-

point, the implicit message was that there would be no unexpected battlefield surprises.

The Plan is Born

In July 1967, the Communist high command, including political and military leaders from both North and South Vietnam, met in Hanoi. Because North Vietnam recalled its foreign ambassadors to attend the meeting, American intelligence learned of the unusual gathering. It could have been the

In the summer of 1967 North Vietnamese warriors and diplomats met in Hanoi and decided to take an immense strategic gamble. While the Tet Offensive was Defence Minister Giap's brainchild, Ho Chi Minh gave his blessings to the effort. His recorded tapes were meant to be played on captured South Vietnamese radio stations. Communist planners believed that everyone would rally to the popular 'Uncle Ho' and help drive out the hated foreigners.

The offensive required a long lead time because of the difficulty of moving supplies south along the tortuous Ho Chi Minh Trail. This section of the supply line consists of a road carved into the side of a hill for the movement of light trucks.

first piece in the intelligence puzzle leading to anticipation of the coming offensive. Instead, analysts believed the meeting's purpose was to consider a peace bid.

Reviewing events, the Communist leaders recognized that heretofore their battlefield strategy had relied upon well-planned, periodic small- to medium-sized surgical strikes against selected targets and daily small-scale actions designed to raise the enemy's anxiety level and destroy his self-confidence. However, aggressive American tactics during 1967 seemed to auger poorly for the future. A Viet Cong general explains:

'In the spring of 1967 Westmoreland began his second campaign. It was very fierce. Certain of our people were very discouraged. There was much discussion on the course of the war – should we continue main-force efforts, or should we pull back into a more local strategy. But by the middle of 1967 we concluded that you had not reversed the balance of forces on the battlefield. So we decided to carry out one decisive battle to force LBJ to de-escalate the war.'

While this statement was written with hindsight, it is doubtful if strategists believed that they could force an American de-escalation so readily. It is notable that aggressive American tactics were producing results and prompted Hanoi to take a huge gamble.

Impatient and concerned over the trend of events, General Vo Nguyen Giap, the North Vietnamese Defence Minister, proposed a general offensive. While it is difficult to ascertain the high command's exact expectations – as of 1989 they remain obscured by propaganda and the difficulty of gaining access to North Vietnamese records – Giap apparently believed that such an offensive would trigger a popular uprising in the South. Hanoi labelled the plan 'the general offensive/general uprising' indicating that they clearly be-

The beginning of the large search and destroy missions in 1967, with their attendant increase in American casualties, coincided with a large increase in racial and civil unrest in the USA. During the first nine months of 1967, public anti-war protest, ranging from minor demonstrations to full-scale riots, occurred in 150 cities. These events drained military resources. The October, 1967 demonstration in Washington, DC, shown here, culminated in the Pentagon Riots. Over 10,000 Marines and Army troops manned positions inside the nation's capital. Three battalions guarded the Pentagon itself. Military planners had to consider seriously the possibility of national insurrection. Such results justified the North Vietnamese emphasis upon relating battlefield events and American public opinion.

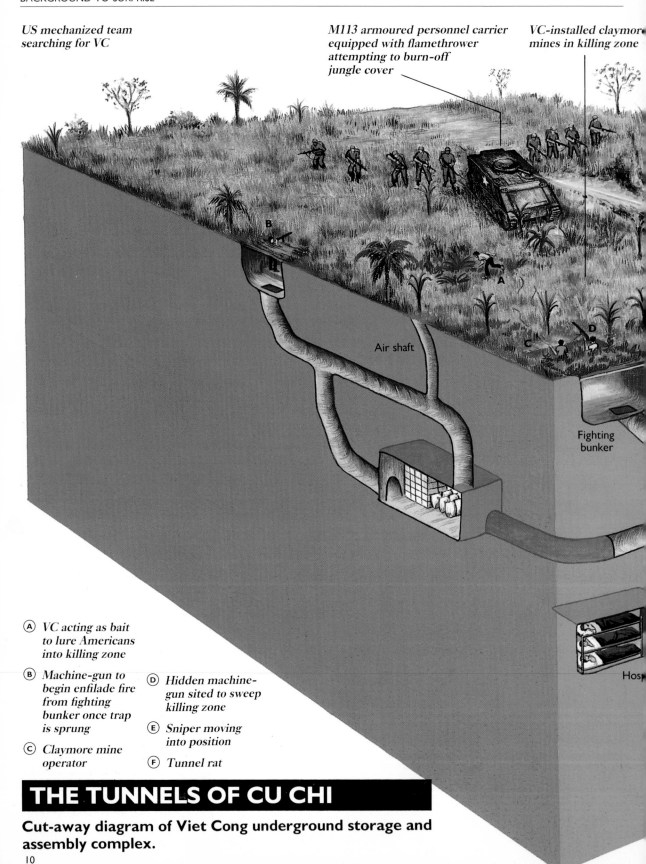

US mechanized team searching for VC

M113 armoured personnel carrier equipped with flamethrower attempting to burn-off jungle cover

VC-installed claymore mines in killing zone

Air shaft

Fighting bunker

Hosp

Ⓐ *VC acting as bait to lure Americans into killing zone*

Ⓑ *Machine-gun to begin enfilade fire from fighting bunker once trap is sprung*

Ⓒ *Claymore mine operator*

Ⓓ *Hidden machine-gun sited to sweep killing zone*

Ⓔ *Sniper moving into position*

Ⓕ *Tunnel rat*

THE TUNNELS OF CU CHI

Cut-away diagram of Viet Cong underground storage and assembly complex.

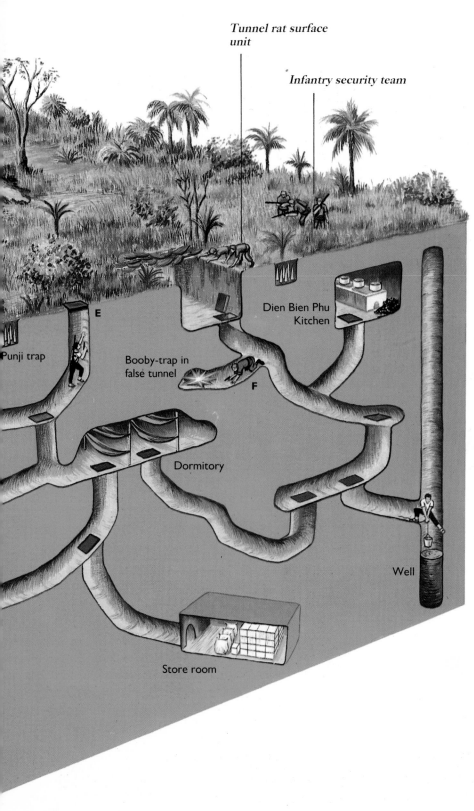

Tunnel rat surface unit

Infantry security team

Dien Bien Phu Kitchen

E

Punji trap

Booby-trap in false tunnel

F

Dormitory

Well

Store room

Twenty miles northwest of Saigon was the Iron Triangle and the adjacent Cu Chi district. Here, since 1945, the Viet Cong and their village sympathizers had laboured to construct an incredible maze of multi-layered, many chambered tunnels. Its existence was a matter of geology, geography and tactics. The soil itself, laterite clay, was ideal for tunnelling since it did not crumble and formed a brick-hard, impermeable surface. The tunnels served as a storage and assembly area. Via a geographic oddity, a protruding finger of Cambodia pointed toward the Iron Triangle and Saigon. Munitions and infiltrating guerrillas moved from sanctuaries in Cambodia to the secure, concealed assembly areas in the tunnels. Allied strategists well understood this and viewed the Iron Triangle as a dagger pointed at Saigon.

However, they failed to appreciate the tactical importance of the tunnels. They had a higher purpose than mere concealment. Communist doctrine decreed: 'If the tunnels are dug so as to exploit their effectiveness fully, the villages and hamlets will become extremely strong fortresses. The enemy may be several times superior to us in strength and modern weapons, but he will not chase us from the battlefield, because we will launch surprise attacks from within the underground tunnels.' Until well past Tet this proved to be exactly the way the VC operated from the tunnels.

The Americans aimed several large-scale search

CONTINUED OVERLEAF

11

CONTINUED FROM OVERLEAF:

and destroy operations at the Iron Triangle, the best known of which, Operation 'Cedar Falls', employed more than 30,000 troops. Literally on the surface, these operations were complete successes: mechanized forces with heavy infantry escorts dominated the above-ground terrain. American officers failed to realize that the absence of the enemy merely meant that he had disappeared underground. The US Army claimed to have destroyed 525 tunnels during 'Cedar Falls', yet the local Viet Cong tunnel inspector noted that only the first 50 metres, at most, of any tunnel was damaged. Given that one village had a 1,700-metre long tunnel system, such destruction was hardly paralyzing. In sum, the sweeps through the Iron Triangle disrupted the Viet Cong, but that is all. As soon as the Americans left, the VC resumed their normal routines. As 1967 drew to a close an important part of this routine involved stockpiling resources for the coming offensive.

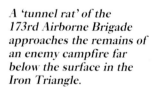

A 'tunnel rat' of the 173rd Airborne Brigade approaches the remains of an enemy campfire far below the surface in the Iron Triangle.

lieved that civilians in the South would rally to their cause. Giap further proposed that the offensive take place during the next lunar New Year festival, some six months hence. The slow, tortuous progress with which supplies could move south dictated this long lead time. While the sacrilege of attacking during Tet might offend many Vietnamese, Giap believed the festival would provide the perfect cover. Furthermore, it had an historic precedent: in 1789 Vietnamese patriots had attacked the occupying Chinese in Hanoi during the lunar New Year festival.

To encourage the fighters in the South, the Communist Party utilized all its formidable propaganda powers. Typical was the exhortation given by the Binh Dinh Province Committee to its trusted cadres:

'The General Offensive will occur only once every 1,000 years.

It will decide the fate of the country.

It will end the war.

It constitutes the wishes of both the Party and the people.'

At secret bases inside South Vietnam and in adjacent, so-called neutral Laos and Cambodia, morale-building efforts proceeded. The 'Second Congress of Heroes, Emulation Combatants and Valiant Men of the South Vietnam People's Liberation Armed Forces' convened to hear Ho Chi Minh's message calling them the 'flowers of the nation'. They included a one-armed soldier who had learned to fire his rifle with his elbow and killed two Americans, and a mine-laying specialist who had been credited with the implausible total of 400 enemy killed, thus earning the title 'Valiant American Killer'. One 17-year-old 'hero' addressed the meeting: 'If he has hatred, even a child can kill Americans.' Such efforts as these rekindled flagging Viet Cong spirits.

Not all the Communist leaders shared the general euphoria. The deputy political chief for Saigon was in closer touch with reality than his higher command. He knew the urban guerrillas were poorly organized and relatively few in number. When he mentioned his doubts, his superiors dressed him down for being 'overly pessimistic' and told him to leave strategy-making to his betters.

In general terms, the July conference in Hanoi decreed that the Tet General Offensive would carry the fighting into previously untouched South Vietnamese urban centres. Here the people would rally to the National Liberation Front and overthrow Thieu's government. Since 1968 was also an election year in America, the successful offensive would help convince the American public that the war was unwinnable. A strike on Saigon was one of the key aspects of the general offensive.

Just as in the Second World War when the German Army secretly advanced through a series of staging areas to suprise the American defenders in the Ardennes, so the Viet Cong brought munitions over the border from Cambodia to the tunnels of Cu Chi and the Iron Triangle. Men and weapons assembled in the tunnels where they received detailed briefings. Systematically they moved into Saigon suburbs and on the eve of the assault gathered in specially prepared safe houses inside Saigon. Agents, often women and children, moved weapons past the city's checkpoints by a variety of subterfuges including hiding them beneath agricultural produce or concealing them inside coffins as part of bogus funeral processions.

Mai Chi Tho, the political commissar of the region encompassing Saigon, carefully planned the assault from a tunnel base in the Iron Triangle:

'During the Tet Offensive, I was in the Iron Triangle. We were working day and night. It was a time of very secret and intensive activity. Many of our officers had to secretly reconnoitre the enemy targets. They moved around in Saigon on forged identity papers. Our fifth columnists, soldiers and officers working inside enemy military installations, came to report.'

From such reports, the Viet Cong received detailed information on the defences they would confront.

The Tet Offensive bore the unmistakeable imprint of General Giap. Giap pursued a three-phase military strategy: resistance; general offensive; and general uprising. The strategy featured an evolution from hit and run guerrilla warfare to the formation of regular units that would engage in conventional, objective-seizing battle. The problem with this doctrine was that it required battlefield concentration and thus provided an unmistakeable target for American firepower.

Communist planners hoped to utilize captured resources in a variety of imaginative ways. NVA artillerymen were to accompany the assault against an Army of the Republic of Vietnam (ARVN) artillery installation in the central highlands. They would man the captured artillery pieces. Similarly, in Saigon, NVA tank troops would follow the assault against an ARVN armour school to operate the captured vehicles. Near Saigon another artillery team would man weapons captured from an artillery training school. Thus the Communist planners boldly schemed to provide their soldiers with the heavy weapons they had always lacked. Meanwhile, another team carried a recorded speech from Ho Chi Minh designed to promote a popular uprising against the South Vietnamese government. They planned on broadcasting this speech once the assault troops had captured the South Vietnamese national radio station.

Private and 2nd Lieutenant (kneeling) of the US Marine Corps. Illustration by Mike Chappell.

MEN, WEAPONS AND TACTICS

The Army of the Republic of Vietnam

Vietnam has a long tradition of resisting outside influence. Opposition to foreigners superseded internecine dispute. Thus, from the beginning it was an unnatural and very uneasy alliance between the South Vietnamese government and the United States. Moreover, what the South Vietnamese government decreed might well be ignored by a people faced with the options of allying with foreigners to fight their own people, staying neutral, or doing whatever it took to survive. Since 1965 American forces had carried the brunt of offensive operations while the South Vietnamese carried out so-called pacification efforts. Thus, on the eve of Tet, they were dispersed in myriad garrisons scattered around the countryside.

Before Tet the South Vietnamese armed forces included 342,951 regulars in the Army, Navy, Air Force, and Marine Corps. Americans performed most technical and command and control functions in these units. Underpinning the ARVN infantry were some 12,000 American advisers. Each division had about 300 Americans who served as liason/advisory/logistics specialists. In the field, each battalion had a three- to five-man American advisory team. Since the Americans brought their own radios, they could rapidly tap into the American arsenal of on-call firepower.

In theory, the American assumption of major combat provided a break from the fighting and thus an opportunity for the South Vietnamese to train and improve. In some cases this is what happened. Nha Trang's excellent Dong De (sergeants' school) is a case in point. More often, soldiers sent to training schools naturally took advantage of the respite from combat to loaf. Furthermore, much of the instruction was poor. A veteran infantryman recalls that Ranger school featured instruction based on outdated US Second World War and Korean War doctrine. Some of the instructors were political appointees. The key instructor position was a patronage post, a welcome, comfortable rear-area assignment. Too often instructors taught American doctrine by rote. In contrast were wounded veterans who would not deal with obsolete doctrine; instead 'they taught wisdom'.

Ironically, by the time the combat schools had updated their curriculum to teach counter-insurgency, the enemy had switched to more conventional, mainforce tactics. Ranger School's 'muddy diploma' – so called because most graduates attended during the monsoon season when combat was at an ebb – and much of the other instruction that was supposed to take place while Americans bore the brunt of combat, failed to achieve American expectations. Part of the problem stemmed from poor equipment. Most ARVN units lacked modern radios, essential for calling artillery and air support. Before Tet, only the élite Airborne battalions and Marine Brigade, one infantry regiment, and five Ranger battalions possessed M-16 rifles. The balance of the ten regular infantry divisions and virtually all the various militias made do with assorted outdated weapons. These units knew they were outgunned when confronting AK-47-firing North Vietnamese regulars or mainforce Viet Cong.

Endemic corruption afflicted many units. Thieu's spoils system kept him securely in power by awarding command positions to cronies, but combat leadership suffered. The common soldier knew that all too often his officers enriched themselves on US aid meant to increase their fighting ability. This situation prevailed even among so-called élite units. Periodically, Westmoreland had to threaten to withhold funds from Ranger battalions, supposedly among the army's best, because they were absconding with massive amounts of aid intended for the civilians they were protecting.

When examining the pre-Tet ARVN order of battle, American planners saw a very uneven picture of performance. Some ARVN units had benefited from withdrawal from front-line combat. Others had lost all combat effectiveness. There were some excellent units, most notably the airborne and marine units. An American adviser said of them:

'These guys are part of the strategic reserve. They get moved all over the country to fight and are away from their families 10 or 11 months a year, year after year. They are all volunteers. When

ALLIED ORDER OF BATTLE

US FORCES AND STRENGTHS, 31 JANUARY 1968
Divisions
1st Marine Division (22,466)
3rd Marine Division (24,417)
1st Cavalry Division (18,647)
  (the Army's best)
1st Infantry Division (17,539)
4th Infantry Division (19,042)
9th Infantry Division (16,153)
23rd (American) Division (15,825)
  (newly formed)
25th Infantry Division (17,666)
101st Airborne Division (15,220)
  (airborne in name only)

Brigades and Other Units
173rd Airborne Brigade (5,313)
199th Infantry Brigade (4,215)
11th Armored Cavalry Regiment (4,331)
5th Special Forces Group (Airborne) (3,400)

Summary
79 Army battalions, 23 Marine battalions, 3,100 helicopters

Allied Forces
1st Australian Task Force (three battalions, about 6,000)
Royal Thai Army Volunteer Regiment (Queen's Cobras) (about 2,400)
Capital (Tiger) Infantry Division (Korean)
9th (White Horse) Division (Korean)
2nd Marine Corps Brigade (Korean)
  Authorized Korean manpower: 42,769
  Actual pre-Tet strength: 48,800

ARMY REPUBLIC OF SOUTH VIETNAM
Airborne Division
  (élite)
Marine Corps
  (two solid 3-battalion brigades)
1st Division
  (the best regular division)
2nd Division
  (problem-prone, high desertion)
5th Division
  (barely effective)
7th Division
  (barely effective)
9th Division
  (the Army's poorest)
18th Division
  (combat-ineffective)
21st Division
  (a good division)
22nd Division
  (adequate, improving)
23rd Division
  (adequate, improving)
25th Division
  (improved after receiving M-16s)
Ranger Battalions
  (uneven, from very good to poor)
Regional Forces
  (151,376 militia)
Popular Forces
  (148,789 militia)
Civilian Irregular Defence Groups
  (42,000 militia)

Total Allied Forces as of 31 December 1967:
1,298,000

people say the South Vietnamese won't fight, they shouldn't include units like the Vietnamese Marines.'

However, in the American estimation, corruption and poor training, leadership, and equipment rendered six of the ten regular divisions combat ineffective.

At the bottom of the pecking order of Allied units were the 42,000 men comprising the Civilian Irregular Defence Groups (CIDG). The task of Training and leading these groups fell to the American and Vietnamese Special Forces. There were two categories of CIDG: Camp Strike Forces (CSF) and Mobile Strike Forces (MSF, familiarly

Paratroopers of the élite ARVN Airborne served as a fire brigade force. The 1st and 8th Battalions, intended for movement north as part of Westmoreland's counter to the NVA buildup along the DMZ, were still in Saigon when the Communists struck. Their fortuitous presence gave the Allied commanders an invaluable hard-fighting reaction force. During Tet, airborne troopers rushed from one emergency to the next.

South Vietnam Military Regions

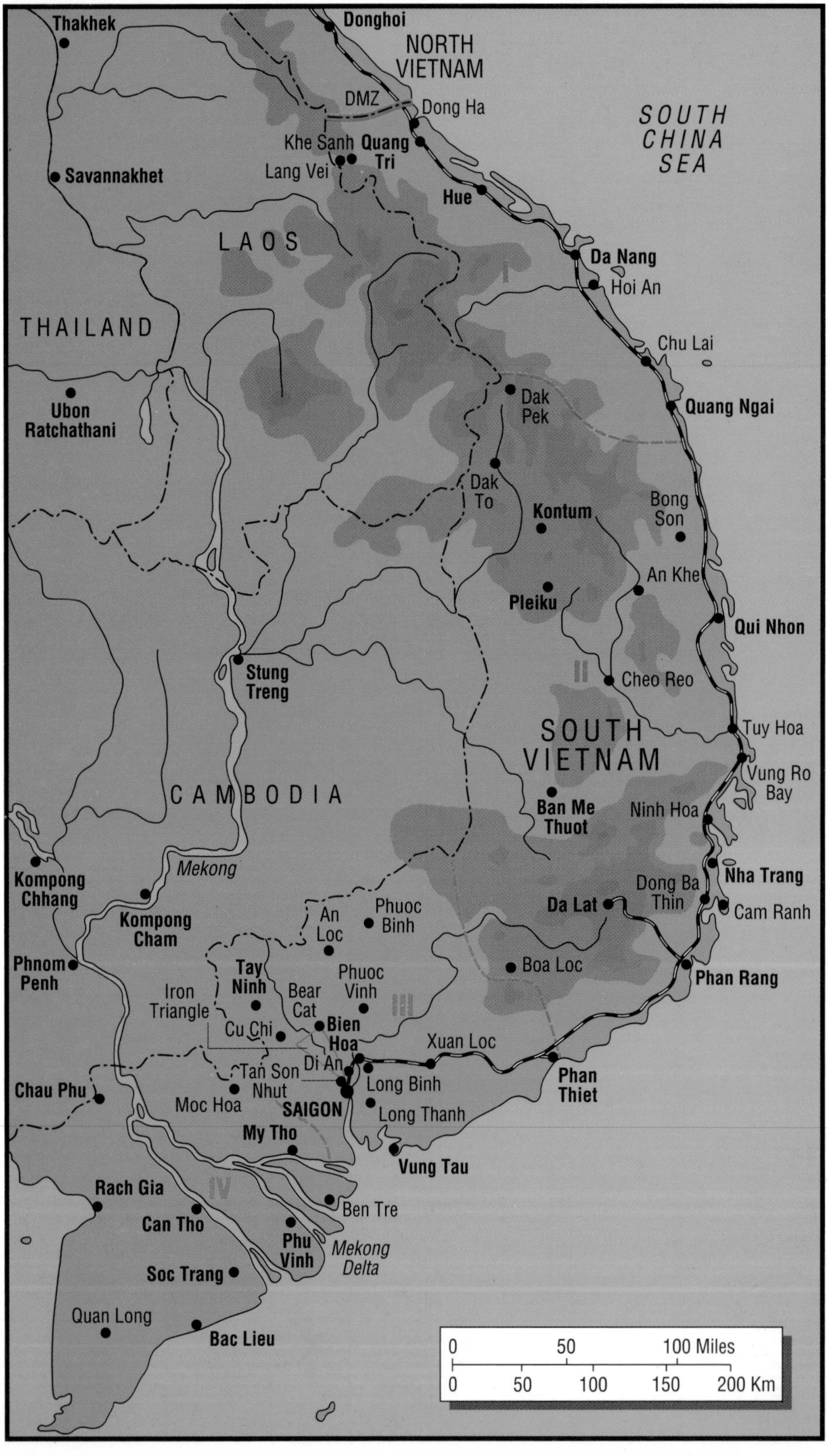

A soldier of the 5th Marine Battalion holds a VC 75mm recoilless rifle round.

Thakhek

Donghoi

NORTH VIETNAM

DMZ

Dong Ha

SOUTH CHINA SEA

Khe Sanh **Quang Tri**

Lang Vei

Savannakhet

Hue

L A O S

Da Nang

Hoi An

THAILAND

Chu Lai

Ubon Ratchathani

Dak Pek

Quang Ngai

Dak To

Kontum

Bong Son

An Khe

Pleiku

Qui Nhon

Stung Treng

Cheo Reo

SOUTH VIETNAM

Tuy Hoa

Vung Ro Bay

C A M B O D I A

Ban Me Thuot

Ninh Hoa

1st ARVN Division radiomen and their American advisers co-ordinate operations with a nearby American Fire Support Base.

Mekong

Kompong Chhang

Kompong Cham

An Loc

Phuoc Binh

Dong Ba Thin

Nha Trang

Da Lat

Cam Ranh

Phnom Penh

Tay Ninh

Phuoc Vinh

Boa Loc

Phan Rang

Iron Triangle

Bear Cat

Cu Chi

Bien Hoa

Di An

Xuan Loc

Tan Son Nhut

Long Binh

Phan Thiet

Chau Phu

Moc Hoa

SAIGON

Long Thanh

My Tho

Vung Tau

Rach Gia

Ben Tre

Can Tho

Phu Vinh

Mekong Delta

Soc Trang

Quan Long

Bac Lieu

0		50		100 Miles
0	50	100	150	200 Km

known as 'Mike Forces'). The former garrisoned the Special Forces' camps while the latter comprised the better trained soldiers (a relative term) capable of active patrolling. A battalion of CSF soldiers, three to five 132-man companies, guarded each camp. Their families usually lived in an adjacent American-built slum put together with nipa palm and stolen materials. In remote situations these camps existed in isolation from normal regional life; in more populous areas they became a centre for people seeking a safe haven. Since one of the goals of the coming offensive was to prove to the people that the South Vietnamese government and its allies could not protect its citizens, the CIDG camps were included on the target list.

The CIDG had limited capabilities. They were at the bottom of the hierarchy for supplies, medical evacuation, fire support, and everything else. Most of their training came from field experience facing 'real' training aids who shot back with superior weapons. However, moulded by the Green Berets, they sometimes accomplished surprising feats. A Special Forces officer has left a description of his men on the eve of Tet:

'These CIDGs were soldiers who would cut up their canteen covers to make green fur collars for

The M-16 was the basic and controversial firearm of the US foot soldier. An automatic rifle, on full automatic it delivered its 20-round magazine in three seconds. To reduce the likelihood of jamming, many soldiers only loaded 18 rounds. Still the M-16 had to be meticulously maintained or else it jammed. The relative merits of the rival automatic rifles were much debated. One VC company commander stated: 'The AK-47 was a good weapon, but most of us carried M-16s.' Asked why, he responded: 'It was so much easier to get ammunition. You were always dropping magazines full of it, or we could buy it from the puppet (South Vietnamese) forces.' A Marine belonging to 'A' Company, 1/1 Marine Regiment, during the Battle of Hue, 9 February 1968.

Every squad included a soldier armed with the M-79 grenade launcher. The M-79 was a single-shot, break-open, breech-loaded shoulder weapon. When loaded it weighed 6.5 pounds. It fired a 40mm grenade to an effective range of 400 yards (while the maximum range of a hand-lobbed grenade was 40 yards). It had a sustained rate of aimed fire of five to seven rounds per minute. Grenadiers carried ammunition in specially designed, pouch-lined jackets. The effectiveness of the 'blooper' gunners made them, along with the radiomen, the first targets in an ambush. A VC captain commented: 'We were very frightened of it . . . A terrible weapon.'

their uniforms; who could struggle all day through thigh-deep mud, carrying half their own weight on their backs without complaint . . . who would bang two B-40 rockets together like indian clubs to see if they would explode . . . who might run under fire; or who might ignore it to carry a wounded American to safety.'

Except for selected CIDG camps, the Communist assault tended to bypass rural areas in favour of city assaults. Thus, the 151,376-man Regional Forces and 148,789-man Popular Forces played a limited part in the Tet Offensive. In the cities the attackers confronted the 70,000-man Vietnamese national police who were forced to play a combat role with which they were unfamiliar and for which they were ill-prepared.

The American Infantry

On the eve of Tet, US forces comprised nine divisions, one armoured cavalry regiment, and two

A CIDG platoon at its base in the II Corps hinterland. Note the many young teenagers that make up this force.

independent brigades. This force had 100 infantry and mechanized battalions numbering 331,098 Army soldiers and 78,013 Marines. The most aggressive of these troops, the Marines, 1st Cavalry Division, 173rd Airborne Brigade, and 11th Armored Cavalry Regiment, were the equal of any of the crack American formations that participated in the two World Wars. The balance were dependable, if unexceptional, soldiers willing to perform their duty.

Writing with the advantage of hindsight, an American officer commented that his country did not acquire ten years' experience in Vietnam, but rather had 'one year's experience ten times'. The reason for this was the rotation system under which a soldier served a twelve-month tour of

US infantryman.
Illustration by Richard
Geiger

Vertical envelopment, landing troops via helicopter behind enemy lines, was a new military concept, first applied during the Vietnam War. In 1965 and 1966, when the Communists first confronted this new weapon, they were taken by surprise and slaughtered in droves. But the helicopter was a mixed blessing. A North Vietnamese general who commanded in the first battles against the US 1st Cavalry Division commented: 'With your helicopters you could strike deep into our rear without warning. It was very effective.' However, 'We were amazed at how dependent you were on helicopters.' The helicopter gave the illusion of control. Troops could land anywhere the terrain permitted, deep within enemy-dominated territory. But once they departed the land reverted to the enemy.

An important part of the American arsenal was the helicopter gunship. A crew chief fires his M-60 at a Viet Cong position.

The gunner's view: in this case friendly soldiers of the 1st ARVN Division sweeping through a hamlet. When targets could be seen, the helicopter gave the Allies what in wars past had been called the 'high ground'.

duty. Every soldier knew to the day his personal DEROS (Date Expected Return Overseas). Most soldiers' prime motivation was to survive until that day. The Vietnam rotation policy differed from previous wars. During the two World Wars sol-diers served for the duration. In Korea, rear-echelon troops served longer than those in combat units. In Vietnam, everyone served the same tour. Typically, for several weeks following arrival in country, a soldier was excited and perhaps looked forward to combat. He lost this enthusiasm after his first engagement. From about the second to the eighth month he performed his combat role dutifully. Then he began to consider himself an 'old soldier' and, like all such, became reluctant to take risks. Often, as a soldier neared his DEROS, sympathetic officers gave him a more secure assignment.

The rotation policy had a major impact on how America fought the war. Rapid manpower turn-over hindered the development of *esprit de corps*. There was a constant influx of green troops

As in most wars, there was not a 'typical' soldier on either side. Because of the difficult jungle ter-rain, field expedients ruled the day. An American foot soldier going on patrol might carry a rucksack stuffed with basic equipment weighing some 50 pounds. In addition, he hefted three days' rations, 500 M-16 rifle rounds, four one-pound fragmentation grenades, two smoke grenades, one or two Claymore mines, 200 rounds for his unit's M-60 machine-gun, three or four canteens of water and his individual weapon. Here, 1st Infantry Division soldiers take a break from a tracking patrol.

Flying from bases in Guam, the B-52 bomber – originally designed for strategic nuclear attack – served as a conventional ground support bomber in South Vietnam. It carried a colossal bomb load, up to 84 750-pound bombs, that could be dropped as close as one kilometre from friendly troops. The B-52 flew so high that it could not be heard on the ground: thus in theory they struck without warning. However, Soviet vessels stationed near the B-52 bases, spies' reports from the heavily infiltrated South Vietnamese command, and careless American security measures frequently gave the intended target advance warning. None the less, B-52 carpet bombing attacks could be devastating and greatly contributed to the defence of Khe Sanh.

Jet strike aircraft provided close support in daylight conditions of good visibility. Because of their speed, the 'fast-movers' were hard targets for enemy anti-aircraft gunners to hit. Although the Americans used a variety of jet aircraft, the Air Force's F-100 Super Sabre was the most common jet used in South Vietnam. It carried up to 6,000 pounds of ordnance.

The NVA/VC had to confront a battlefield fact of life: they invariably faced vastly superior American firepower. They constantly sought ways to compensate by using every possible strategem conceivable by a very inventive people. These ranged from pre-battle morale/political indoctrination to post-battle evasion and retreat tactics.

A captured NVA regular wears the characteristic Ho Chi Minh sandals and pith helmet. Heavy Tet losses among southern-born Viet Cong shifted the war's burden to the northern regulars.

replacing combat experienced men. Since the likelihood of encountering the enemy was somewhat random, a newly arrived soldier had about the same chance of engaging in hard combat as did an experienced soldier. A North Vietnamese officer commenting on why America lost said: 'One weak point was your rotation of soldiers. You were strangers here anyway, and as soon as someone began to learn the country you sent him home.' Thus, from the soldiers' standpoint, the major morale factor was the rotation policy. He knew the war would not be won during his tour of duty, so

he reasonably asked 'why try?'. His patriotic and self-sacrificial tendencies competed with instincts for self-preservation. For him: 'The end of the war was marked by the individual's rotation date and not by the war's eventual outcome – whether victory or defeat.'

The rotation policy also had an adverse impact on the officer corps. Knowing their time was limited, many officers selfishly sought to enhance their careers during their Vietnam service. This was the infamous 'ticket punching' behaviour so criticized after the war. The officer's goal was not to win the war, but to acquire a good fitness report for his file. Furthermore, career officers strove to serve six months in a combat unit and six in a staff position. This combined experience gave them the best chance for future promotion. Yet it had a serious adverse impact on operations in the field. Just about the time an officer became experienced enough to lead effectively, he switched jobs. A new commander brought new procedures, and everyone constantly had to change, adjust and relearn all aspects of combat. This was a serious disadvantage, particularly against a foe who had fought a lifetime on the same ground.

The fundamental miltary challenge confronting the Americans and their allies was that, despite unprecedented mobility provided by helicopters and APCs, they infrequently contacted the enemy unless he wanted the contact. The Tet Offensive changed this. The enemy massed his forces and tried to hold his ground.

The Communists

Communist forces fell into two distinct groups: the North Vietnamese Army (NVA) regulars and the Viet Cong (VC). At the war's beginning, the southern-born Viet Cong operated in true guerrilla style without support from the NVA regulars. As the war intensified, increasing numbers of North Vietnamese made the perilous march south along the Ho Chi Minh Trail to join the fighting. American intelligence estimated that at the time of the offensive, about fifty per cent of the 197 mainforce enemy battalions in the south comprised NVA regulars. At all times, the Hanoi high command dominated their southern brethren. The

Typical soldier of the Viet Cong. Illustration by Mike Chappell.

The AK-47 was the standard hand-held firearm on the Communist side. The Russian-designed gas-operated automatic rifle fired a 7.62mm round. It had an effective range of 400 metres and delivered 30 rounds per magazine. Ruggedly built, it was believed by many American soldiers to be greatly superior to their own M-16. In contrast to earlier wars where foot soldiers fired rifles, the AK-47 turned every enemy infantryman into a light machine-gunner. A young Viet Cong soldier carries the Chinese version of the AK-47.

escort replacements back south. A disabling wound was the only other ticket home. As the war dragged on, more and more recruits saw orders sending them south as a death sentence. Yet they went, and, in sharp contrast to American policy, the NVA soldier served for the duration. As one envious American general expressed it: 'Charlie had no DEROS.'

Compared with the Allies, the NVA lived an extremely primitive life. Their health suffered accordingly. A typical NVA prisoner reported that while everyone took malaria pills, due to their poor physical condition, 70 men in his company had contracted the disease by the time of his capture.

It was also a life lacking comfort and pleasure. While during the march south through Laos and Cambodia they occasionally met women at communications and liaison stations, once they neared the combat zone they seldom made contact with the opposite sex. Each evening a political officer harangued the men. He told of combat heroes and of great past and future successes against the ARVN and Americans. Typically, a commissar might acknowledge the strength of American aircraft and guns while stressing the moral superiority of the NVA/VC. Although political indoctrination was an important component of orthodox Communist training, at least one veteran reported that it often failed to stimulate the troops for a most basic reason: the political officer did not accompany the men on combat missions and thus was discredited. Periodically travelling entertainment troops arrived to enliven the soldiers' lonely routine. While their arrival was welcome, particularly if the troop featured women, their departure only highlighted the men's isolation. The life of an NVA soldier was one of tremendous physical and emotional deprivation.

Within the Viet Cong were two levels of combatants: mainforce (called regular by the Americans) units that numbered about 60,000 men organized into regular combat units, and the paramilitary or guerrilla forces. The latter, in turn, comprised regional, or territorial, guerrillas and local guerrillas. Main force units engaged in full scale combat and were veteran, skilled fighters. The paramilitary units provided logistical support, scouts and guides, and engaged in hit and

NVA's objective was to reunify Vietnam: the Viet Cong – fighting under the banner of the National Liberation Front – had the slightly different goal of obtaining a monopoly of political power in the south. American intelligence had identified seven North Vietnamese Army divisions in South Vietnam by the beginning of 1968. They numbered about 50,000 soldiers. Additional NVA regulars served in mainforce VC units.

Until the war's end, a North Vietnamese soldier sent south returned home only in one of two circumstances. If he belonged to the small cadre held out of battle to reconstruct a battered unit (a practice similar to that used by assault troops in the First World War) he would return to

Up until the Tet Offensive, the Viet Cong and North Vietnamese avoided battle except on ground of their own choosing. Usually they tried to draw the Americans into a prepared killing ground that featured well-camouflaged, deeply-dug trenches, bunkers and spider holes. Experienced American officers learned to avoid assaulting unknown numbers of enemy soldiers in prepared positions. Instead, they preferred to fall back and call in air strikes and artillery. However, the imperative to report a sizeable 'body count' drove some aggressive leaders to costly and foolish attacks. The 173rd Airborne's assault on hill 875 in 1967 and the Hamburger Hill action in 1969 were two dismal examples. A trench/tunnel complex uncovered by the 173rd Airborne Brigade.

A captured VC sapper reported: 'You had lots of wire around Polei Kleng but it was easy to get through. I just don't think you have a defensive barrier that is effective against us.' At Hue, a spearheading sapper company formed four 10-man teams equipped with two B40 and one B41 rocket launchers as well as AK and CKZ rifles with 200 rounds of ammunition. Each sapper also carried 20 explosive charges to breach fortified defences. Nearly naked, to avoid tangling in wire, a former VC sapper demonstrates infiltration technique.

The Soviet RPD machine-gun fired the same ammunition as the American M-60. However, at 10.5 pounds it was less than half as heavy as its counterpart. It was cap-able of firing 900 metres, 200 metres less than the M-60, but this seldom mattered in situations where combat ranges typically were less than 20 metres.

run ambushes and mine laying. While it is exceedingly difficult to reconstruct the Communist order of battle – it was a source of great debate at the time within Westmoreland's headquarters – on the eve of Tet, some 400,000 paramilitary fighters were present.

The fundamental problems confronting the Communists are well-expressed by the commander of the 2nd Viet Cong Division: 'When the Americans entered the war, we spent all our time trying to figure out how to fight you. The incredible density of your firepower and your mobility were our biggest concerns.'

Communist Weapons and Tactics

Both the Viet Cong and the North Vietnamese lacked the heavy weapons of their opponents. They essentially operated as light infantry. Since they could not compete with American firepower, they developed a variety of compensatory tactics. Analysis of the initial encounters with the Americans led to the following conclusion according to a Viet Cong general: 'The way to fight the American was to grab him by his belt, to get so close that his artillery and air power was useless.' The Communists had rediscovered the 'hugging' tactics used by the Germans during the Second World War.

Secondly, the Communists had to counter American mobility. A North Vietnamese general explains how this was done:

'Our mobility was only our feet, so we had to lure your troops into areas where helicopters and artillery would be of little use. And we tried to turn those advantages against you, to make you so dependent on them that you would never develop the ability to meet us on our terms – on foot, lightly armed, in the jungle.'

Often such jungle combats featured the VC/NVA fighting from entrenched positions. If they chose to fight outside fortified areas, the Communists tried to strike hard and fast and then

Regular soldier of the NVA. Illustration by Mike Chappell.

Russian-manufactured rocket-propelled grenades (RPGs) were the descendants of the very successful Second World War German hand-held anti-tank weapons. Nominally effective up to 500 yards, in combat the NVA and VC employed RPGs at much closer range. RPGs could penetrate up to 250mm-thick armour, easily an overmatch for the M-113's 35mm-thick plating. RPGs and rockets took a terrible toll of Marine Corps tank troops during the street fighting in Hue.

withdraw before American firepower intervened. Usually they sought to engage American units who were moving and were thus more vulnerable. Despite all these tactics, if it came down to a slugging match, the VC/NVA could not compete with American firepower. One NVA combat veteran estimated that 70 to 80 per cent of all NVA losses came from artillery and airstrikes.

The NVA/VC always prepared meticulously before launching an assault. Operations typically began with a careful reconnaissance of the object-ive. The recon unit, comprising the best soldiers, moved close to the Allied position and then dispatched two- or three-man teams to move in as close as possible to scout the objective. The recon

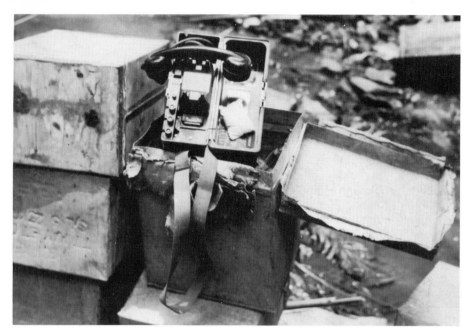

Poor communications forced the Communist attackers to adhere to plans. Such inflexibility caused heavy losses when rapid American counter-measures placed reserves between the attackers and their objectives. In Saigon, in particular, initial Communist successes degenerated into unco-ordinated small unit actions. Only at higher command levels did the Communists have field telephones (shown here) and radios.

unit paid particular attention to the positions of the defenders' heavy weapons. Upon its return to base, the recon unit diagrammed the objective for the sappers who were to spearhead the assault. The sappers were the second most élite soldiers in NVA units. Frequently, assault troops constructed a sand table of the hostile position. Each unit studied the table and then rehearsed its role. In preparation for infiltrating Allied positions, every-one received instruction in disarming mines and trip flares. In actual assaults, élite sapper units led the way. Even the most formidable-seeming positions proved porous against the Communists' skilled infiltration abilities.

For the Tet Offensive, most objectives were in urban areas. A prisoner explained the scouting procedures used here:

'In our reconnaissance of cities, we are norm-ally met by local force liaison people at a pre-arranged location within or close to the city. The liaison people escort us to the exact positions or locations to be attacked. If there are several ARVN soldiers in the area, we usually disguise ourselves as ARVNs. But in cities where there are only a few ARVN soldiers, we wear civilian clothes.'

The Communists took advantage of the Christmas truce for a final reconnaissance. The commander of the 9th Viet Cong Division, for example, personally inspected his unit's primary objective, Tan Son Nhut Air Base outside Saigon, while one of his regimental commanders visited 'the family grave site' at a military cemetery just outside the base.

Because the VC/NVA units lacked modern communications, officers could not adjust plans to changing circumstances. Thus assault units re-ceived rigid orders to follow the attack plan. A prisoner recounts:

'All units must go by this plan and a soldier must execute an order even if many get killed. They must launch the attack at all costs. The plan always shows how to get into the objective area, where key points to be destroyed are located and how best to exfiltrate.'

In another tactical departure, many attacking units at Tet had no prepared withdrawal routes.

It was a point of discipline and pride always to try to carry away the wounded and the dead. This practice led to the frustrating experience of an Allied unit fighting an intense combat, taking losses, and after the battle finding little to indicate if the enemy, in turn, had suffered.

In the absence of artillery, heavy fire support had to come from rockets, recoilless rifles and mortars. Mortars included 82mm and 120mm weapons. The latter type was a most formidable weapon. Based on Soviet design, the 120mm mortar had a range in excess of four miles. A five-

A captured 82mm mortar on right stands next to a US 81mm version. The Communists could fire American ammunition even though the tube was slightly larger. Mortar and rocket bombardment heralded most of the initial Tet attacks.

The lightly armed Viet Cong had to find alternatives to compensate for their lack of firepower. They relied heavily upon mines and booby traps. A VC document analysing American tactics stated: 'US troops clumsy and vulnerable to booby trapping and mining.' Mines inflicted about half the damage and destruction American armour suffered. Mines and booby traps caused 10 per cent of US fatalities and 15 per cent of wounds between 1965 and 1970. Furthermore, their presence served as a substantial tactical brake on ground operations. When a trap exploded to kill or maim, the infuriating knowledge that local civilians knew the location of nearby booby traps sometimes drove the survivors to commit savage atrocities.

man crew served the weapon and could break it down into three loads to carry it through even the most rugged terrain.

The mortar attack had been a staple of Viet Cong tactics since the war began. Relying upon careful reconnaissance, a mission made easier by the near total lack of concealment of important posts within an Allied installation, the mortar crews prepared concealed firing sites and calculated firing angles before the bombardment began.

Thus they were able accurately to 'walk' their rounds across a base's important installations in a short, intense bombardment. This bombardment both inflicted losses and forced the defenders to keep their heads down. While the defenders were hunkered down, élite sappers spearheaded the effort to breach the defences.

Far less accurate were the free-flight 107mm, 122mm and 140mm rockets. Rockets had figured prominently in Russian Second World War tactics,

Two approaches to fortifications: an American-built firing bunker defends the vital Long Binh base area, an important target for the Tet Offensive. Such positions were easily plotted by VC recon detachments.

In contrast, a VC bunker built to withstand direct hits from artillery and bombs is extremely well camouflaged.

so it is not surprising that the Russians supplied rockets to their allies. The rocket's great merit was that it efficiently delivered a large explosive charge to the target. A 90-pound rocket, transported in two sections, could be carried to its launching site and propel a 35-pound charge to a target 10 kilometres distant. It required a conventional howitzer weighing some 3,300 pounds to equal this firepower. Thus the rocket had a much superior warhead-to-weight ratio. On the down side, rockets were inaccurate. They were useless for hitting discrete targets. Accordingly, Communist gunners employed rockets as area bom-

bardment weapons, particularly against airfields and ammunition dumps, and to deliver sudden, stunning saturation fire to cover an assault. Nationwide, the typical first warning that the Tet Offensive was underway came when mortar rounds and rockets exploded on defensive positions.

Only along the DMZ did the North Vietnamese Army employ tube artillery. In late 1967 it hauled Russian-designed 130mm field guns into fortified firing positions and began the long-range bombardment of Marine positions. To American generals, this was reminiscent of Dien Bien Phu, and was one more factor drawing their attention north as the Communists prepared for the real assault elsewhere.

In spite of this calculus, the Communist high command's plan called for its soldiers to switch their tactics completely. For the first time in the war, they were to capture and hold selected objectives throughout the country. To do this they had to mass – and this would provide unmistakeable targets for US firepower.

On the Eve

When it was all over, it seemed that American intelligence officers had had the pieces of the puzzle in their hands but had been unable to assemble a clear picture of enemy intent. As early as 29 October 1967, the Viet Cong 273rd Regiment had attacked a small district capital and, contrary to normal practice, tried to hold it. They suffered terribly when the inevitable massive Allied air and artillery bombardment drove them out. Intelligence officers could not understand why the enemy risked certain heavy losses for a meaningless objective. With hindsight they understood that the Communists were practising urban assault tactics.

Similarly, in November four NVA regiments fought a bitter 22-day campaign around the obscure border town of Dak To. The Americans redeployed the equivalent of a division to defeat the assault. Captured documents revealed that the attack had been designed to 'force the enemy to deploy as many additional troops to the Western Highlands as possible'. The scheme worked, though again at heavy cost. The American troops had vacated positions around some of the urban objectives specified for the Tet Offensive.

There were other tell-tale signs: a flurry of attacks in Dinh Tuong Province where historically the Viet Cong tested new tactics; a sharp decline in Communist desertion rates (the troops were being told that victory was near); prisoner statements that the entire country would be 'liberated' by Tet. By December 1967, high-ranking American officers had begun to believe that the Communists would try a major offensive in the near future. America's top soldier, General Earle

RVN National Police Field Force enlisted man, Saigon. Illustration by Mike Chappell.

Wheeler, Chairman of the Joint Chiefs of Staff, addressed the US public on 18 December, twenty-three years and two days after the surprise German assault in the Ardennes, to say that 'there may be a Communist thrust similar to the desperate effort of the Germans in the Battle of the Bulge'.

Wheeler's warning came from the analysis performed by Westmoreland and his staff, who had been carefully studying captured documents. These clearly described a change in Communist strategy. Accordingly, the general informed Washington that the Communists intended 'to undertake an intensified countrywide effort, perhaps a maximum effort'. The administration responded by speeding up the schedule of troop movements to Vietnam, but that was all. Except for Wheeler's statement, which had little impact, the Johnson administration chose not to reveal Westmoreland's analysis to the public and did nothing to brace the

The basic armoured vehicle of the war was the M-113 armoured personnel carrier (APC). Combat experience quickly showed the need to increase the armour and firepower of the APC. Technicians bolted extra armour along the sides to protect against RPGs, belly armour to shield against mines and an armoured cupola for the commander's .50cal machine-gun. The addition of two side-mounted M-60 machine-guns converted the vehicle to the Armored Cavalry Assault Vehicle. Mechanized units used the ACAVs as light tanks. They had surprising cross-country ability. The combination of mobility and firepower demonstrated to the high command that armour could usefully contribute to the war. Westmoreland wrote: 'The ability of mechanized cavalry to operate effectively in the Vietnamese countryside convinced me that I was mistaken in a belief that modern armor had only a limited role in the fighting in Vietnam.'

American people for the coming blow. Having spent the past months claiming great progress, policy makers – military and civilian alike – refused to reverse course. They persisted in painting a rosy picture and by this decision played right into Giap's hands.

On 5 January, the US Mission released documents captured on 19 November 1967, which included an order to the People's Army:

'Use very strong military attacks in co-ordination with the uprisings of the local population to take over towns and cities. Troops should flood the lowlands. They should move toward liberating the capital city [Saigon].'

Yet the attached analysis provided by the mission, apparently reflecting the prevailing belief in Westmoreland's headquarters, was that these orders were 'ambiguous' as to the time fixed for the attack and possibly represented 'internal propaganda' designed to inspire the enemy's troops.

When the South Vietnamese General Staff later studied the Tet Offensive they hit upon the

essential basis for the intelligence failure. Having been taught American doctrine, they were primarily concerned with the Communist 'capabilities and not his intentions'. Capabilities could be quantified, and it was clear to all the Allies that the enemy could not hope to capture and hold urban objectives. Therefore, intelligence officers dismissed all indications that the enemy intended to try anyway.

A second major factor beyond the inability of military intelligence to assess accurately the signs of enemy build-up accounts for the Tet Offensive's surprise. When the American high command examined their strategic maps at the beginning of 1968, they focused on the northernmost provinces bordering the so-called demilitarized zone (DMZ) that separated North and South Vietnam. Since mid-1967, Westmoreland had been shuffling strength northward in response to the enemy's growing strength. By the New Year he had positioned a tremendous amount of available military resources there. The positions included a

series of fortified, but isolated, Marine Corps posts along the DMZ. The high command, and President Johnson in particular, feared that a major assault across the border and from neighbouring Laos might turn one of these bases into a Dien Bien Phu. Mid-January patrol actions seemed to confirm the high command's worries: two dug-in NVA divisions had surrounded the Marine Corps combat base of Khe Sanh. In sum, by January 1968, enemy pressure had over-stretched American resources. Distracted by the threat in

By the beginning of 1968, the Allies had assembled a considerable armoured force. The US Army's contingent included the famous 11th Armored Cavalry Regiment, seven divisional cavalry squadrons, seven mechanized battalions, two tank battalions and an independent tank company, and five cavalry troops supporting light infantry and airborne units. The Marine Corps also had considerable armoured assets. The crack 1st Australian Task Force provided an APC troop. Ten South Vietnamese armoured cavalry squadrons were available.

An aerial view of Khe Sanh. Communist pressure against this base caused Westmoreland to divert increasing strength to the northern I Corps region. With hindsight, it appears he was duped by a skilful Communist diversionary build-up.

General Fred Weyand sensed too many troops were deployed along the Cambodian border. He urged Westmoreland to recall them to positions closer to Saigon. This redeployment proved to be Westmoreland's best decision before Tet.

Major General Charles Stone (back row, third from right) carefully prepared defensive plans in case the Communists struck. His care paid great dividends in the defence of Pleiku.

the north, the US high command seriously under-estimated the enemy's potential for major, nation-wide attacks.

Major General Frederick C. Weyand commanded the American field forces in III Corps Tactical Zone. His command stretched from Saigon out to the Cambodian border. According to Westmoreland's recent strategy, 39 of his 53 manoeuvre battalions were operating against enemy bases along the Cambodian border. Unbeknown to Weyand, as the Americans shifted out from the urban area, the Communists marched in. However, radio intercepts and the lack of contact with the enemy in the border area alarmed Weyand. On 9 January he telephoned Westmoreland to explain his concern and to recommend that forces return from the border. In a key decision, Westmoreland agreed. When the Communists struck, the number of American battalions within the urban zone had doubled. Their presence made a tremendous difference.

Elsewhere, as January progressed, disquieting signs of enemy build-up continued and they too prompted countermeasures. Early in the month, the 4th Division in the Central Highlands captured a plan for an attack on Pleiku. In mid-January, 101st Airborne captured plans for an attack on the province capital of Phu Cuong.

However, the Communist practice of compart-mentalizing planning paid dividends. Since neither of the plans mentioned anything except the immediate activities of the units involved, American intelligence officers failed to foresee that they were part of a nation-wide plan. Consequently, counter-measures were left to local commanders. On 26 January the 4th Division commander, Major General Charles Stone, assembled all area commanders and prepared a co-ordinated response should an attack take place. His foresight stands in sharp contrast to that of other commanders. He also moved a tank company to Pleiku as a mobile reserve. Similarly, a few days later, Westmoreland ordered the 4th Cavalry Squadron to relocate near Saigon's Tan Son Nhut airbase. He reckoned that 'they would provide a ready mobile reserve with impressive firepower'. Both of these small shifts helped when the attack came.

By January, Westmoreland had become sufficiently alarmed to request that the South Vietnamese cancel the coming Tet cease-fire. On 8 January the chief of the South Vietnamese Joint General Staff, General Cao Van Vien, told Westmoreland that he would try to limit the truce to 24 hours. A week later, President Thieu argued that to cancel the 48-hour cease-fire would adversely affect his nation and its soldiers. He agreed to limit

Downtown Saigon on the eve of the decisive Tet Offensive.

the ceasefire to 36 hours, beginning on the evening of 29 January. The South Vietnamese government promised to announce the change one day before it was to take effect. In the event it failed to make the announcement in a timely, useful way. In the IV Corps region south of Saigon, for example, the order cancelling the Tet ceasefire reached headquarters shortly after 10 p.m., a mere four and a half hours before the attacks began.

The Americans did little better. During the day of 30 January Westmoreland's headquarters issued a warning directing that 'Troops will be placed on maximum alert with particular attention to the defense of headquarters complexes, logistical installations, airfields, population centers and billets.' This warning covered the prime targets of the impending assault, yet it either came too late or was largely ignored.

So, heedless of coming crisis, the South Vietnamese prepared to celebrate their lunar New Year. The celebration's peak would come on the night of 30 January. The official ARVN history describes the nation's mood:

'A relative lull seemed to be prevailing all over South Vietnam . . . leaves were readily granted the troops for the lunar New Year and measures were taken by the Administration to give the common people as normal a Tet as possible . . . The people had forgotten about the dying war. They wanted to celebrate Tet with as much fervor as in the old days.'

During the night of 30 January revellers swarmed the streets of Saigon to greet the New Year of the Monkey. Soldiers belonging to the local garrison had not received word the authorities had cancelled the truce. But everyone knew that the ban on fireworks had been lifted for the holidays, so the explosions of thousands of traditional fire-crackers rocked the air. Slowly, as Viet Cong assault forces moved from their safehouses into attack position – some of the 67,000 committed nationwide in the first wave – the sounds of combat replaced the sounds of festival.

TET SAIGON

Assaults on the Urban Centre

The Communist plan sent 35 battalions against six primary targets in the Saigon area. Their objectives were the headquarters of the South Vietnamese Joint General Staff (JGS); the Independence Palace, which served as President Thieu's office; the American Embassy; Tan Son Nhut Air Base; the Vietnamese Navy headquarters; and the National Broadcasting Station. Eleven battalions, comprising about 4,000 mostly local men and women, assaulted the city's urban centre. The C-10 Saigon Sapper Battalion, numbering about 250 men and women who were very familiar with Saigon – many worked as *cyclopousse* or taxicab drivers – spearheaded the attacks. They were to hold the objectives until additional local force battalions arrived to reinforce them.

Shortly before 3am, the guard outside the government radio station saw a small convoy stop and disgorge a group of armed men dressed in South Vietnamese Riot Police uniforms. An officer briskly approached him and announced the reinforcements had arrived. The guard responded: 'I haven't heard anything about it.' Then the officer shot him.

Years earlier, Viet Cong agents had purchased a house 200 yards from the radio station. There they had stockpiled arms and ammunition for future operations. When the soldiers assigned to attack the radio station broke out the stored weapons they found termites had eaten through the wooden gun-stocks. Undeterred, they improvised by wrapping rags around the weapons and proceeded with the mission. The well-organized attackers broke into the station while a machine-gunner provided covering fire from a nearby apartment building. His accurate first sweep killed most of the platoon of ARVN paratroopers who lay sleeping on the roof. A North Vietnamese radio

specialist followed the assault wave into the station. His job was to play a pre-recorded tape of Ho Chi Minh announcing the liberation of Saigon and the beginning of the General Uprising. He had detailed diagrams of the station layout and duplicate keys provided by an agent on the station's staff.

A wounded VC fighter and a female nurse captured by ARVN rangers in Saigon during the 'Mini-Tet' attacks in the summer of 1968. Similar civilian-clad local VC spearheaded the attacks at Tet.

The foresight of the ARVN lieutenant colonel in charge of the station thwarted these plans. The previous afternoon this officer had arranged to take the station off the air if an attack came. Upon hearing gunshots, a technician sent the coded signal and power to the station was cut off. The attackers held their objective for six hours, but were unable to broadcast Ho's message.

The 34 sappers assigned the Independence Palace employed the same commando-style tactics

The Assault on Saigon

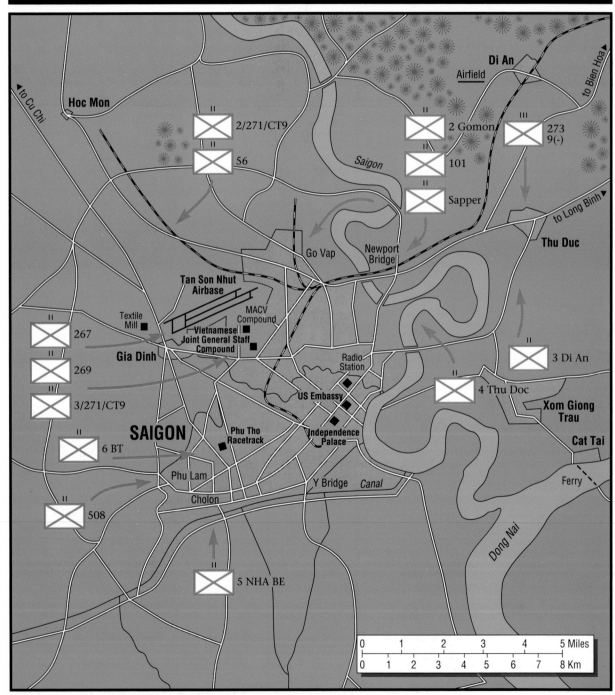

as would be used against the American Embassy. At 1.30am a B-40 rocket exploded on the staff entrance gate. The sappers rushed toward the objective. However, the Palace was one of the best defended sites in all of South Vietnam. The Palace security force, comprising the presidential guard, national and military police and two tanks, were far too strong for the attackers. Repulsed, they retreated into a nearby building. Such was their discipline that they held out for two days in a futile last-ditch stand. Thirty-two died during this operation.

Against Navy headquarters the Communist high command had devised a complicated plan intended to capture both headquarters and nearby docked ships. The ships would then be used to transport people from rural areas to Saigon to participate in the General Uprising. In pursuit of this ambitious scheme, twelve sappers blew a hole in the security wall but were unable to make more than a brief penetration. Within five minutes, ten were dead. Here, as often the case nationwide, the attackers had been told to seize the objective and hold until reinforcements arrived. Also, as fre-

quently proved the case, the reinforcements did not exist.

The attack against the JGS compound began at 2.00am. Just as the sappers began their assault on Gate Number 5, an American Military Police patrol jeep appeared. The attackers engaged the jeep, and this pause allowed the ARVN guard to close the gate and prepare a defence. Additional American MPs assisted the defenders and the first assault collapsed. The Communists intended a local force unit, the 2nd (Go Mon) Battalion, to attack Gate Number 4 at the same time, but the assault units were delayed during the approach march. They were not in position until 7.00am. Amazingly, against a thoroughly alert defence they managed to penetrate the JGS compound. But these attackers made the same mistake committed by the sappers who assaulted the American Embassy. Instead of capitalizing on their success – which in this case meant overrunning the virtually undefended nerve centre of the entire South Vietnamese military – they dug in and awaited reinforcements. As prisoners later revealed, the attackers blindly adhered to the pre-battle plan

ARVN soldiers of the 30th Ranger Battalion fight in Saigon on 31 January.

and thought they had accomplished their mission when they seized a building clearly marked 'General Headquarters'. In fact, this building was only one of several command buildings, and not the most important.

The failure of initiative allowed an American helicopter to deliver President Thieu to the compound at about noon. Thieu used the command facility as an emergency headquarters. He bravely conducted meetings even while fighting raged about half a mile away. Eventually ARVN airborne and marine units rooted the Go Mon battalion out of the JGS compound. The attackers had come very close to achieving a striking success.

The South Vietnamese had always been sensitive about an American presence in the cities. Bowing to these sensitivities, as a gesture of confidence in ARVN competence, and because of a belief that the Communist threat had diminished, in mid-December the US Command had yielded to the ARVN full responsibility for the close-in defence of Saigon. Thus, only the 1,000-man strong 716th US Army Military Police Battalion (MP) guarded more than 130 American installations in the greater Saigon area. In spite of the alert, only some one-third were at their posts when the VC struck. A mere 25 of the 300 Vietnamese MPs were on hand to assist them.

The hole in the embassy wall through which 19 VC entered the compound.

Soldiers of the 716th Military Police Battalion across the street from the still-occupied American Embassy.

The 716th MP Battalion's Message Log for the first two hours of the offensive described the widespread, surprise VC attacks:

0300: BOQ No. 3 reports enemy action
0315: US Embassy under attack
0316: Explosion at Phoenix City BOQ
0317: Explosion at Townhouse BOQ
0318: BOQ No. 1 under attack
0319: McArthur BOQ under attack
0321: Report of hostile attack at Rex BOQ
0325: Explosion at BOQ No. 2
0340: Automatic-weapons fire and attack at BOQ No. 3
0341: MPs at US Embassy request urgent ammo resupply
0342: Heavy sniper fire at Metropole BEQ
0350: Incoming mortars at Montana BEQ
0358: Saigon port area reports small-arms and automatic-weapons fire
0359: Mortars and rockets fired at US Embassy; reinforcements requested
0407: MP jeep C9A reports that 2-ton truck carrying 25-man reaction team to BOQ No.3 hit by rockets and claymore mines. Heavy casualties
0408: Jeep C9A hit; both MPs killed
0419: BOQ No. 3 pleads for ammo resupply
0420: General Westmoreland calls; orders first priority effort to recapture US Embassy
0430: Request armored vehicles and helicopters for embassy assault

The damaged side entrance to the embassy and the symbol of tattered American prestige.

Combat sequence at Bachelor Officer Quarters No. 3. During the night the first reinforcements arrived via truck, hit a claymore mine and suffered heavy losses.

Chancery Building

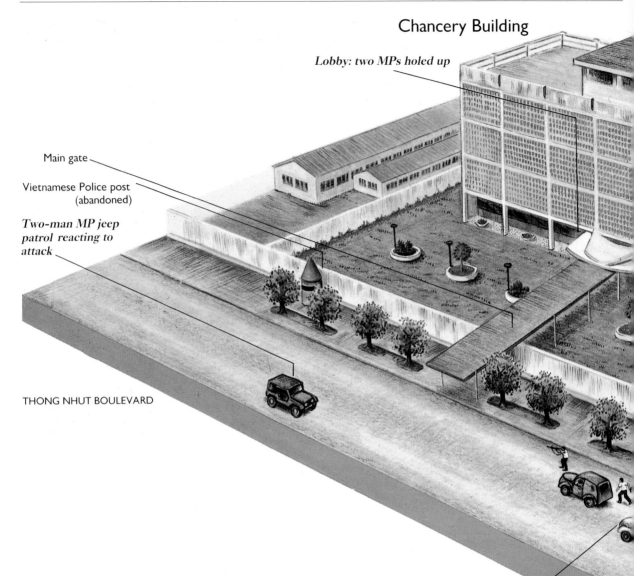

Lobby: two MPs holed up

Main gate

Vietnamese Police post (abandoned)

Two-man MP jeep patrol reacting to attack

THONG NHUT BOULEVARD

VC truck and taxicab

Breach blown in wall

At a rundown automobile repair shop five blocks from the American Embassy, 19 sappers belonging to the C-10 Battalion boarded a small Peugeot truck and a taxicab to begin the short drive to their objective. A South Vietnamese policeman spotted the vehicles moving without lights. He chose to avoid trouble and so did nothing. The vehicles turned onto Thong Nhut Boulevard where they encountered the embassy's outer layer of protection provided by four more South Viet-namese police. They too fled without firing a weapon. The vehicles proceeded along the second line of defence, an eight-foot high wall that surrounded the embassy compound. Approaching the night gate, they encountered two American MPs. Although attacks had been taking place throughout Saigon for more than an hour, such was the state of inter-allied communication that the embassy defenders had no idea the Communists had broken the truce. Amid an exchange of gunfire, the MPs backed into the compound and shut the steel gate, thus sealing the embassy from the outside world. At 2.47am a guard radioed the signal that the embassy was under attack.

Meanwhile, out in the street, the attackers unloaded weapons and explosives. One VC used a satchel charge to blow a three-foot hole in the wall. Displaying formidable courage but poor tactics, both VC officers led the way through the breach. The explosion had alerted the two guards. They whirled around and shot down the officers. One shouted into his radio: 'They're coming in! They're coming in! Help me! Help me!' It was his last message. With their burst of accurate fire the two MPs had eliminated the enemy leadership; but they too soon died in the return fire.

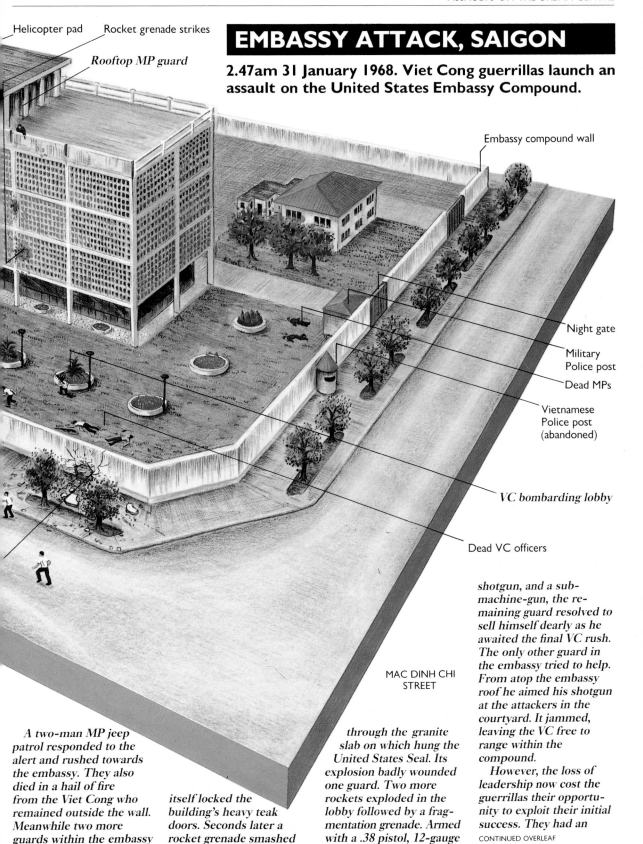

Helicopter pad   Rocket grenade strikes

Rooftop MP guard

EMBASSY ATTACK, SAIGON

2.47am 31 January 1968. Viet Cong guerrillas launch an assault on the United States Embassy Compound.

Embassy compound wall

Night gate

Military Police post

Dead MPs

Vietnamese Police post (abandoned)

VC bombarding lobby

Dead VC officers

MAC DINH CHI STREET

A two-man MP jeep patrol responded to the alert and rushed towards the embassy. They also died in a hail of fire from the Viet Cong who remained outside the wall. Meanwhile two more guards within the embassy itself locked the building's heavy teak doors. Seconds later a rocket grenade smashed through the granite slab on which hung the United States Seal. Its explosion badly wounded one guard. Two more rockets exploded in the lobby followed by a fragmentation grenade. Armed with a .38 pistol, 12-gauge shotgun, and a sub-machine-gun, the remaining guard resolved to sell himself dearly as he awaited the final VC rush. The only other guard in the embassy tried to help. From atop the embassy roof he aimed his shotgun at the attackers in the courtyard. It jammed, leaving the VC free to range within the compound.

However, the loss of leadership now cost the guerrillas their opportunity to exploit their initial success. They had an

CONTINUED OVERLEAF

47

CONTINUED FROM OVERLEAF:

ample supply of C-4 explosives to breach the embassy itself. Only a handful of lightly armed Americans remained in the building. Instead, the VC milled about in confusion and eventually took position behind the shelter of some convenient oversized flower tubs. From this position they exchanged gunfire with targets of opportunity. Outside the walls American reinforcements began to arrive. VC fire kept them from entering via the gate. In the dark they failed to see the hole in the wall. For the rest of the night it was a stand-off.

Reserves, following an ARVN V-100 armoured car, tried to work up the alley to rescue the wounded at the truck. Heavy fire drove off the armoured car.

More South Vietnamese and US reinforcements arrived to resume the advance.

*MPs pinned down by
heavy VC fire.*

*Resistance finally
crumbled and VC
suspects were removed.*

0449: Cleveland and Columbia BOQ request ammo and assistance

0550: Three claymores detonated at Saigon motor pool.

Booby traps discovered.'

Shortly after the first alert, the commander of the 716th implemented the 'disaster plan'. Designed for such emergencies as riots or isolated bombings, it was woefully inappropriate for the chaos of combat sweeping through Saigon. Jeeps and open-topped trucks, such as those mentioned in the 0407 and 0408 entries above, rushed to respond to the dozens of emergencies. Their bravery mattered less than their lack of firepower and training. By dawn the VC had made major penetrations into western and southern Saigon and controlled large areas in the suburb of Cholon.

The widespread attacks such as those described in the 716th's Message Log typically featured a handful of attackers. However, initial reports could not assess the size of the enemy forces. To the American officer commanding the Saigon area, General Weyand, it was difficult to make sense of the multiple enemy thrusts. The fact his own headquarters was under rocket and ground attack also hampered tactical judgment. The map showing the reported attacks around Saigon reminded him of 'a pinball machine, one light after another going on as it was hit'. Between 3am and 5am he shifted some 5,000 mechanized

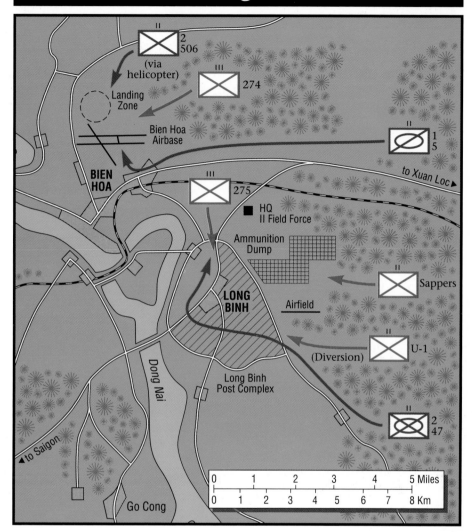

The Bien Hoa - Long Binh Area

Soldiers of the 2/47th Battalion (mechanized) assault VC positions in the Long Binh area.

and airborne troops to defend the various installations under assault. His rapid, yet considered reactions limited enemy success.

Cavalry to the Rescue

Fifteen miles north of Saigon was the Long Binh logistical and command complex. This sprawling base area, which extended to the enormous Bien Hoa Air Base, was a target too big to overlook by Communist planners. At 3.00am an intense rocket and mortar barrage pelted the area. The veteran 275th VC Regiment assaulted Long Binh's northern perimeter while a local VC battalion launched a diversionary attack against the eastern bunker line. Meanwhile VC sappers infiltrated the huge ammunition dump just north of Long Binh. Simultaneously, the 274th VC Regiment attacked Bien Hoa.

While well-coordinated and bravely driven home, these attacks fell victim to superb American mobility and firepower. Half an hour after the opening barrage, the 2/47th Battalion (mechanized) began a speed march from Bear Cat toward Long Binh. At first light the 2nd Battalion/560th Infantry airlifted into Bien Hoa Air Base. The élite 11th Armored Cavalry Regiment, the Blackhorse Regiment, made a twelve-hour forced march to arrive at Long Binh during the day. Once in position, the multiple machine-guns of the mech-

Some of the VC killed by the APCs of the 9th Infantry Division.

anized units' APCs shot apart all Viet Cong attacks. Perhaps above them all was the performance of the mechanized cavalry troop of the 9th Infantry Division.

At bases north-east of Saigon, the radio net of 1/5 Armored Cavalry, 9th Infantry Division, came alive at 6am on 31 January. The squadron learned

Descended from Second World War tanks, the M-48 medium tank served as the mainstay of the American armour during the Vietnam War. A crew of four, comprising a commander, gunner, loader and driver manned the tank. Its armament consisted of a 90mm gun, a 7.62mm machine-gun by the commander's cupola, and a .50cal machine-gun by the *loader's cupola. With a top speed of 30mph, it had surprising 'jungle busting' cross-country ability. Although heavily armoured, tanks sacrificed their mobility and thus proved vulnerable in urban combat. A Patton belonging to the 11th Armored Cavalry supports operations on 2 February around Bien Hoa.*

that large enemy forces were attacking Tan Son Nhut, Bien Hoa, Long Binh, and Saigon itself. Officers paid particular attention to news from Long Binh, where one of the Division's mechanized battalions had been sent the night before. By listening to that battalion's tactical radios, the squadron anticipated that soon it would be needed. One hour later came the order for Troop A to move out.

Amid great confusion, the squadron commander ordered the troop, minus one-third of its strength left behind to garrison a fire-support base, to begin a speed march to Bien Hoa. Hardly had the troop left its base than it ran into an ambush. The VC had skilfully anticipated American reactions, but they underestimated the cavalry's mobility and firepower. The troop drove through the ambush while laying down a carpet of fire from their ACAVs. Without suffering serious damage, Troop A cleared the fire zone only to encounter a mile-long strip of houses each one of which seemed to conceal an enemy gunner. Beginning to take losses, the troop managed to speed through the gauntlet.

The column's lead tank came to a small concrete bridge and rolled across it without incident. Suddenly an explosion rocked the air and the bridge collapsed in fragments. The troop's ACAVs managed to ford the stream, but the balance of the heavier tanks had to remain behind. Troop A entered the city of Bien Hoa where it found the central square crowded with people. It pushed through the throng, but suddenly the troopers realized that the 'crowd' was actually several companies of enemy soldiers. The enemy simultaneously realized that they confronted American armour. The Viet Cong's initial volleys disabled two ACAVs. More ACAVs entered the square and opened fire with all their weapons. They drove the VC to cover, pushed the knocked-out vehicles aside, rescued their crews, and pressed on for the airbase. The column now comprised one tank and eight ACAVs.

The reassuring words of the squadron commander filled the radio. From an overhead helicopter he directed the cavalry through the byzantine labyrinth of narrow streets. Nearing the air base he spotted hundreds of enemy soldiers

M35A2 'gun truck' of 27th Transportation Battalion. Illustration by Peter Sarson and Tony Bryan.

belonging to the 274th VC Regiment lining Highway 1, apparently deployed to stop any relieving column. His warning saved the column. Exploiting its mobility, the cavalry left the highway and drove a parallel route. The ACAVs' machine-guns shot up the unsuspecting enemy from the rear and finally reached the beleaguered air base.

Its presence at Bien Hoa provided the narrow margin between victory and defeat. Along with the 2nd Battalion/506th Infantry, it repulsed all assaults. By day's end its one tank had been hit nineteen times and the crew replaced twice. Of the twelve ACAVs that began the mission, only six still ran by nightfall. The troop had suffered heavily, but the survivors felt elation that after months of being the target of ambushes without being able to hit back, it had finally met a stand-up enemy and inflicted terrible losses upon him.

A cavalry officer describes his unit's feelings on the first day of February:

'I can still remember the feeling of pride we had in our operations center the next morning when we heard the squadron commander's initial report . . . that Saigon, Bien Hoa, and Long Binh were literally ringed in steel . . . Five cavalry squadrons had moved through the previous day and night, converging on the Saigon area. When dawn broke, they formed an almost-continuous chain of more than five hundred fighting vehicles . . . We actually cheered . . . from that morning the outcome was never in doubt. We knew that our enemy could never match our mobility, flexibility, and firepower.'

The Press Reaction

Within fifteen minutes of the first attack, an Associated Press (AP) reporter had typed out the first bulletin announcing the attack. By a twist of fate that was to have immense consequences, the embassy was close to the quarters housing the Western Press. This allowed reporters to rush to the scene of the action. The resultant concentration of the Press undoubtedly distorted the significance of the combat. Because they could not see over the walls, neither they nor the soldiers knew what was going on inside. Consequently they relied upon the excited comments of one of the MPs who was outside the walls. This MP stated: 'They're in the embassy.' When a reporter asked an MP captain for confirmation, he replied: 'My God, yes . . . we are taking fire from up there . . . keep your head down.' This information was sufficient for AP to send a bulletin stating:

'The Vietcong seized part of the US Embassy in Saigon early Wednessday . . . Communist commandos penetrated the supposedly attack-proof building in the climax of a combined artillery and guerrilla assault that brought limited warfare to Saigon itself.'

This bulletin arrived just before the first-edition deadlines for very influential morning newpapers in the eastern USA. Headline writers quickly updated their papers and spread the shocking message that the enemy had captured the symbol of American prestige.

In Saigon, the American command failed to appreciate the importance of the embassy combat. The commander on the spot was quite content to wait for daylight before proceeding. He knew he had the VC cornered. At higher command levels the numerous actions exploding all over the country seemed to demand more attention. Responding to pressure from Washington, around 5am Westmoreland had Weyand send a helicopter with a platoon of airborne soldiers to land on the embassy roof. Automatic weapons fire from the surviving VC drove it off. To avoid unnecessary risks, the higher command decided to wait for daylight before trying again. By the time the helicopter returned, MPs had forced the embassy gate. They easily killed the few surviving VC. What an American participant called 'a piddling platoon action' was over after a six hour combat.

Reporters swarmed the grounds as military spokesmen tried to explain what had happened. Controversy centred on whether the VC had actually entered the embassy. Although they had not technically entered the embassy building, the AP stood by their opposing claim. Too often reporters had been deceived by official pronouncements. AP's insistence that the VC had entered the embassy further undercut the credibility of official statements and set the stage for one of the most memorable visual images in this, the world's first television war.

At 9.20am, Westmoreland arrived at the just-secured compound dressed in an immaculately pressed and starched uniform and held a hastily arranged Press conference. In America viewers saw a scene of carnage. Dead VC sappers littered the embassy grounds, their bodies sprawled

A dead VC next to a landscape planter inside the embassy compound. His rocket launcher and equipment lie nearby.

around the flower pots. Blood, death, and battle damage abounded. In the midst of an embassy apparently under siege, the general explained that the the enemy never penetrated the embassy itself. He exuded confidence and claimed the allies were returning to the offensive.

A Washington Post reporter recalls: 'The reporters could hardly believe their ears. Westmoreland was standing in the ruins and saying everything was great.' An AP reporter later explained that, given the record over the years, 'we had little faith in what General Westmoreland stated.' When the American public read their morning papers they received two impressions: the Viet Cong had seized the embassy itself; and Westmoreland was lying when he said they had not. The pyschological damage done to the American war effort would become clearer in the coming weeks.

The Phu Tho Racetrack

In spite of complete surprise and the initial success of many of the opening assaults, on the Communist side events were not proceeding as desired. There was no general uprising and little active civilian support in Saigon. In order to preserve secrecy, the VC units that attacked Saigon had little knowledge of the overall picture. Most had received the briefing that they were to take part in an attack of unspecified dimensions. However necessary for security reasons, this secrecy prevented all unit co-ordination. Thus, while achieving numerous isolated initial successes, once in position the VC had to fend for themselves against a growing Allied counter-attack.

Repulsed or evicted from their six prime objectives, the attackers broke down into small units and took shelter in buildings throughout Saigon. In particular, the attackers clung to the Phu Tho racetrack area. The 6th BT VC Battalion had seized the racetrack during its opening assault. Communist planners valued this objective because it was the hub of several major roads, possession of its open terrain denied the Allies a potential landing zone for helicopters bringing reinforcements, and it provided an easily recognized rallying place for rural VC unfamiliar with Saigon.

The first warning of the enemy build-up in the Phu Tho area came at 4.45am when a 716th MP jeep patrol radioed: 'The driver caught a slug in the gut and I'm under heavy automatic weapons fire. Can you give me some help?' Then the radio

Westmoreland at the Embassy on the morning of 31 January.

A burned out M-113 on the Phu Tho racetrack. The APC was hit by VC rocket fire.

As late as 10 February, US reinforcements, including these soldiers of the 199th Light Infantry Brigade, were still reinforcing the Phu Tho position. The trucks are parked on the running surface.

Dead Viet Cong on perimeter of Tan Son Nhut Air Base, 1 February.

went dead. Before help arrived the two MPs had been killed.

A company from the 199th Infantry Brigade (Light) boarded trucks and APCs and headed for the racetrack at 8.00am on 31 January. Six blocks from the objective it met heavy automatic weapons fire from rooftops and buildings lining the road. A VC rocket struck the lead APC killing the platoon leader and two crew. VC rifle, machine-gun, and grenade fire hammered the column as it slowly advanced towards the racetrack. When heavy enemy fire repulsed its first charge, the infantry regrouped and tried again. Supported by helicopter gunships and recoilless rifle fire, they captured the racetrack by 4.30pm. At dusk a reinforcing company landed on the racetrack itself and the Americans prepared a defensive perimeter.

Over the next several days additional reinforcements arrived, including the 33rd ARVN Ranger Battalion, and together the Allies expanded their control to the areas adjacent to Phu Tho. It was not easy. An American mechanized company, driving through a narrow street three blocks away, suddenly was hit by a VC rocket and machine-gun ambush. The opening barrage destroyed the two rearmost APCs and heavily damaged a third. However, its crew stood by their guns to provide covering fire while the accompanying infantry dragged the dead and wounded clear of the kill zone. Then the survivors hustled back to the racetrack itself just in time to help repulse a large-scale VC counter-attack. The fighting ebbed and flowed around Phu Tho for several more days. Eventually, every Viet Cong unit that participated in the Saigon offensive contributed manpower to this battle.

As early as 1 February, COSVN, the Communist high command, realized that many elements of its grand plan had miscarried. While complimenting its soldiers for their performance, it sent out orders that called off further assaults against fortified Allied positions. Furthermore, it criticized faulty co-ordination and liasion and noted serious tactical shortcomings. None the less, not until 7 March, five weeks after the first attack, did ARVN Rangers finally clear the entire capital city of Saigon.

AVRN Ranger, Saigon. Illustration by Mike Chappell.

TET COUNTRY-WIDE

Surprise at Da Nang

While the Saigon and Hue battles monopolized most attention from Allied commanders and the Press, fierce Communist assaults took place all over South Vietnam. Here ARVN and militia forces bore the brunt of the ground defence. Part of the ferocity derived from the briefings given to many of the assault troops. They were told that they were engaged in an offensive that was to lead to a general uprising. In keeping with this brave talk, about half the assault units did not receive any instructions regarding a withdrawal in the event of unforeseen circumstances.

While South Vietnamese authorities failed to disseminate word of the cancelled truce in Saigon, in the smaller provincial and district towns some units were on full alert. This made a great difference when the Communists struck. After the event, high-ranking South Vietnamese and American officers would claim that official policy called for holiday leaves for only ten per cent of all manpower. In fact, a much more liberal policy was in effect. Typical was the 7th ARVN Division, which had 4,000 men present and 3,500 on leave when the attack came.

The first assault wave utilized local VC units, sappers, and in-place agents. The Communist attacks strove to disrupt further South Vietnamese improvements by targeting headquarters, training and logistical bases. Every attack also featured an assault against the local radio station. Just as in Saigon, the attackers carried tapes to broadcast in hopes of stirring up the popular uprising. In general, the attacks' success depended upon two conditions: were the defenders alerted with leaves cancelled and in position; were the Americans able to bring their heavy firepower to bear even at the risk of civilian losses?

The abortive assault on Da Nang, the coun-try's second largest city, demonstrated this point. A police agent who had infiltrated the local VC organization warned of the coming blow. None the less, a reinforced company briefly penetrated the headquarters of the South Vietnamese I Corps on the city outskirts. When the dashing corps commander, Lieutenant General Hoang Xuan Lam, first heard from a staff officer that an assault was under way he responded incredulously: 'Baloney, baloney!' Assured that it was true, he drove through enemy fire to reach his headquarters at dawn. Assessing the situation, Lam tapped the map with his swagger stick and spoke to his U.S. adviser, Major P.S. Milantoni:

'Milantoni, bomb here. Use big bombs.'

'General, that's pretty close.'

'Bomb.'

The adviser requested the mission only to be told by another American officer that the mission was so close to friendly positions that it would never get clearance. Milantoni replied: 'General Lam just gave it.' The bombs struck a mere 200 yards from I Corps headquarters. The VC fire diminished and Lam ordered more strikes. When the VC pulled back, the South Vietnamese general sent helicopter gunships in pursuit. The VC attack on Da Nang failed.

Battle in the Delta

The Mobile Riverine Force (MRF) was a special American brigade-sized outfit equipped for the unique combat conditions in the Mekong Delta. It moved through the myriad rivers and canals aboard assault boats and possessed numerous improvised weapons such as 60-foot long monitors armed with a revolving armoured turret housing a 40mm cannon intended for close fire support. It had specially designed floating artillery barges to provide heavier firepower. All of these weapons and more were attempts to solve the constant problem of the Vietnam War, how to find and fight an elusive enemy who usually revealed himself only when his first shots announced an ambush. When the Tet Offensive exploded in the Delta, the problem was not locating the enemy. The Viet Cong seemed to be everywhere.

In the Mekong Delta, the Communists assaulted thirteen of sixteen provincial cities. Such was the ferocity of their attacks that Allied intelligence soon identified all except one battalion listed on its order of battle. In other words, the Communists were sending in all their men. Furthermore, captured plans revealed a notable absence of the customary contingency plans for retreat. Apparently the attackers planned to hold their ground. The MRF, on the other hand,

manned dispersed positions along waterways in an effort to interdict VC supply lines. Units had to concentrate hastily before counter-attacking VC penetrations in various urban settings.

Their first call was to My Tho, south of Saigon. Three VC battalions and a sapper company had entered the city while one battalion remained on the outskirts. Two MRF battalions hastened to the city to support the units of the embattled 7th ARVN Division. It took three days to recapture My Tho. The battle featured tough house-to-house fighting, a type of combat very different from the MRF's normal mission and one unsuited to its special weaponry. Like a fire brigade, once it had secured My Tho, MRF units rushed to other threatened positions including Saigon itself.

Few American units operated in the heavily populated Delta region south of Saigon. The notable exception was the joint Army/Navy Mobile Riverine Force (MRF). Built around two brigades of the 9th Infantry Division, the MRF had unique assets suitable for the labyrinth of rivers, canals and rice paddies characteristic of the Delta. In most of Vietnam, the Allies used helicopters to reach the enemy in otherwise inaccessible terrain. In the water-logged Delta, the Allies employed specially designed water-craft. They included armoured troop carriers known as Tango boats after their call sign. The Tango boat featured stand-off armour designed to detonate RPG or recoilless rocket rounds before they hit the boat's armour. Used as assault craft, the Tango boats glided through the shallows to land infantry on dikes and levees.

The heavy fighting during Tet strained the services of the flying ambulances. Using the famous call sign 'DUST OFF', pilots time and again took extreme risks to rescue the wounded. Their dedication, coupled with superior hospital facilities gave wounded Americans and their allies an unprecedented survival rate. Over the entire war, the average time-lapse between wounding and hospitalization was less than one hour. Consequently, 99 per cent of all American wounded who survived the first 24 hours lived. Pilots and crew paid a stiff price for their gallantry. During Tet's 12-day period of nation-wide fighting, they evacuated more than 8,000 wounded. Forty of the total of 64 operational 'DUST OFF' helicopters were hit.

The VC made the mistake of attacking Chau Phu, a provincial capital on the Cambodian border. Opposing them were some of the roughest fighters in all South Vietnam. They included small but deadly teams of the Special Forces Detachment B-42, a Project PHOENIX recon unit, and Navy SEALs shown here. These élite men recaptured Chau Phu in a bitter 36-hour combat that caused many civilian losses and destroyed a quarter of the city.

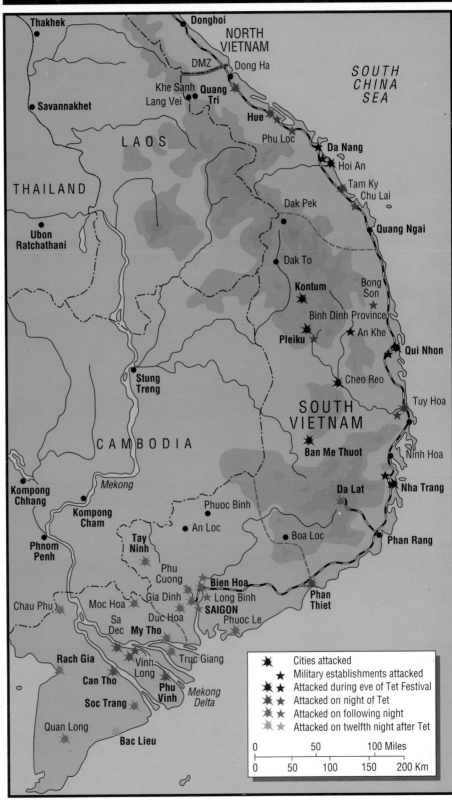

Targets of the Tet Offensive

Legend:
- ★ (black star burst / black star) Cities attacked / Military establishments attacked
- Attacked during eve of Tet Festival
- Attacked on night of Tet
- Attacked on following night
- Attacked on twelfth night after Tet

0   50   100 Miles

0   50   100   150   200 Km

A scout dog team belonging to the 4th Infantry Division flushes out enemy snipers still clinging to Kontum five days after the Communists attacked the city.

In the war against the French, the Vietminh had successfully recruited sympathizers by entering urban areas and forcing the French to employ heavy weapons to drive them out. They then blamed the civilian losses on the French. By occupying churches, pagodas, schools and hospitals, the Communists created the same dilemma for the Americans during the 1968 Tet Offensive. Vietnamese civilians return to their destroyed homes near Bien Hoa on 2 February.

For an unprecedented thirty consecutive days the Mobile Riverine Force fought without rest. Its contributions were key to the many tactical successes gained in the Delta. General Westmoreland, taking a typical American view that undervalued ARVN fighting, said afterwards: 'The MRF saved the Delta.' Indeed, its stout fighting justified the Presidential Unit Citation it earned. Still, here as elsewhere, tactical success could not conceal the hard truth that the Viet Cong had demonstrated to the civilian population of the Delta that, despite American support, they could strike anywhere, anytime. Since ultimately the war would have to be won or lost through the effort of the South Vietnamese, this demonstration contributed to Communist strategic victory.

An MRF boat captain well understood the consequences of the Tet Offensive in the Delta: 'After Tet this whole country really changed.' Speaking of a town badly damaged in the fighting, he continued: 'The VC really tore the place up and I think the Americans more or less got blamed for it. We had to evacuate the town and when we did go back . . . there were quite a few Vietnamese people around who kind of looked down on us a little for leaving them.' Supporting this captain's analysis was the experience of the Mekong Delta river city of Ben Tre, which was home to some 35,000 civilians. A reinforced VC regiment numbering about 2,500 men attacked and gained substantial footholds within the city. To evict the Viet Cong, the Allies had to summon artillery and air strikes. This caused extensive damage to the city and produced one of the most memorable quotes of the war. While explaining what had taken place to a reporter, an American major said: 'It became necessary to destroy the town to save it.' The American Press played this quote to the hilt, using it to epitomize the seeming futility of the war effort.

The Central Highlands

Fierce fighting also took place in the twelve central provinces. Major ground attacks struck seven provincial capitals and three other objectives. At Qui Nhon, a coastal city in II Corps area, before the attacks began, the ARVN defenders discovered the Communist plan when they captured eleven VC agents. But such was the muddle within South Vietnamese units at Tet that Communist sappers assaulted exactly as revealed and still seized their objectives. The attackers even seized the jail, where they captured the ARVN captain who had directed the successful raid that had bagged the eleven agents.

Typical was the battle of Ban Me Thuot in the Central Highlands. Here the 23rd ARVN Division had captured a plan for an attack on the city on about 20 January. The divisional commander, Colonel Dao Quang An, accordingly cancelled his unit's Tet leave. He put out patrols six miles from the city, and these patrols ambushed elements of the 33rd NVA Regiment as they were moving into position. None the less, the fighting at Ban Me Thuot raged for three and a half days, with the ARVN soldiers taking heavy losses because of their inexperience in city fighting. Reluctantly, An decided he had to employ artillery and air strikes despite the resultant civilian devastation. Yet the battle continued for a solid nine days, the city centre changing hands four times before the 23rd ARVN Division regained control. An's leadership greatly impressed the Americans. An adviser

Captured .50cal machine-gun and Soviet-made rocket launcher mounted on stand. In background are two captured flags.

Having suffered terrible losses, the VC reverted to more economical tactics. A Vietnamese C-47 destroyed in the artillery attack on Tan Son Nhut Air Base the night of 17/18 February.

Another victim of the artillery attack at Tan Son Nhut, a F-4C Phantom II.

commented that had he not decided to cancel Tet leaves and to deploy far-ranging ambush patrols, the city would have fallen. Further, the adviser told MACV that An's tactical handling of the battle had been flawless.

In sharp contrast was the conduct of the major general commanding in the delta. When the attack struck he was at his fortified headquarters protected by tanks and armoured infantry. He did not emerge for days, leaving his American advisers to conduct the defence. Similarly, the ARVN colonel commanding at Vinh Long cracked under the strain of events. When an American officer reported helicopters receiving fire and asked permission to return fire, all he received was a blank stare. Another adviser found the province chief wearing civilian clothes under his military uniform – just in case.

Despite heavy fighting in many places, Allied units regained control in most provincial cities within a week. On 7 February, NVA tanks spearheaded an assault that overran the Lang Vei Special Forces Camp near Khe Sanh. With hearts in their throats, the American high command wondered if this were the start of the long-expected attack on Khe Sanh. Perhaps it was just another diversionary attack against a convenient and exposed target, because the Communist high command chose not to try to exploit this success. On 17-18 February the Viet Cong created a brief stir when they made artillery assaults against Allied installations throughout the country. But in comparison with the initial operations, these were low effort/low risk harassing affairs. After the first week sustained combat took place only in Saigon and Hue.

By 21 February, the VC/NVA high command faced battlefield reality. Their assaults had been extremely costly and had failed to achieve the predicted success. Accordingly, COSVN issued orders for its units still in contact around the cities to retreat. There were to be no more ground assaults on fortified Allied installations. Instead, COSVN ordered units to revert to hit-and-run tactics characterized by mortar and rocket bombardment and sapper raids. COSVN made one exception – the units in Hue were to hold their positions.

Typical soldier of the North Vietnamese Army. Illustration by Mike Chappell.

BLOODY HUE

The Imperial City of Hue was the most venerated place in Vietnam. The stone walls of its inner citadel had been built with the aid of the French in the 1800s. Peking's Forbidden City had served as the model for Hue's citadel. Thus it was a place full of gardens, moats and intricate stone buildings. Standing above the citadel was the highest flagpole in South Vietnam, as such, the most visible symbol of the South's struggle for independence. Communist planners did not overlook what was, with the clarity of hindsight, such an obvious target.

The war had not touched Hue, yet it was more than a symbolic target. A rail and highway bridge crossed the Perfume River and continued north. They served as the main land supply routes for the growing number of Allied troops along the DMZ. Hue also served as a major unloading point for waterborne supplies that were brought from Da Nang on the coast.

The attackers possessed very detailed information about Hue. They had divided the Right Bank into four tactical areas and had pinpointed nearly every civil and military installation. Viet Cong intelligence officers had prepared a priority list of 196 targets and had listed individuals to be captured. The plan called for their evacuation if possible; otherwise they were to be killed. In addition, 'Cruel tyrants and reactionary elements' – categories encompassing most South Vietnamese officials, military officers, politicians, Americans and foreigners except the French – were to be separated, taken outside the city and 'punished' – meaning killed. The Viet Cong carefully laid the groundwork for what became their most horrific atrocity.

On 30 January, a US Army radio intercept unit overheard Communist orders calling for an attack on Hue that night. Following standard procedure, it forwarded the message through channels. The Hue defenders did not receive the message in time. It was another in a long list of intelligence failures relating to the Tet Offensive.

Inside the city, Brigadier General Ngo Quang Truong, the commander of the 1st ARVN Division, had received Westmoreland's alert calling for cancellation of the cease-fire. Considered one of the best South Vietnamese generals, Truong gathered his staff at his HQ compound and kept them on 100 per cent alert. This vigilance paid dividends when the enemy attack struck. But over half his division's manpower still received holiday leave. Furthermore, given Hue's record as an 'open' city, Truong did not think the Communists would attack the city itself. He positioned his battalions to defend outside the urban area. Here too was a failure in preparation.

When the attack came, the only regular garrison comprised the all-volunteer Hoc Bao (Black Panther) Reconnaissance Company, 1st ARVN Division. They guarded Truong's HQ in the northern corner of the citadel. Scattered throughout the rest of the city were support troops. Across the Perfume River was the South Side, where a Military Assistance Command Vietnam (MACV) compound housed American and Australian advisers and staff. These two strongpoints were to become islands of resistance when the 12th VC and Hue City VC Sapper Battalions, two NVA infantry regiments, and a rocket battalion flooded the city.

Surrounded by rows of thick-walled masonry houses, with many streets too narrow to permit access by Marine armour, the Citadel at Hue was a difficult position to even approach. Tall trees and hedgerows limited visibility to 25 yards. With two weeks to prepare, the defenders dug hundreds of camouflaged, mutually supporting positions rendering the Citadel an extremely tough objective. The old fortress and flag tower, from where the Communist banner flew during the long battle.

At 2am, 31 January, one of Truong's outlying patrols reported at least two enemy battalions advancing on the city. Apparently the Tet-induced torpor prevented him from making much use of this warning. In any event, he did not notify his allies at the MACV compound. They first learned of the enemy's presence an hour and forty minutes later when a dozen 122mm rockets detonated in their compound. Additional rocket and mortar bombardment provided preparatory fire while local VC, who had already infiltrated Hue dressed as civilians, took up positions to await the arrival of NVA assault troops hurrying into the city.

The Communists mistimed their first assault on the MACV compound. Instead of following on the heels of the rockets, they waited some five minutes. This gave the defenders just enough time to gather weapons and man defensive positions. A brave army soldier purchased another five minutes by manning an exposed machine-gun position atop a 20-foot wooden tower built on the compound's walls. His fire stopped the first rush of some forty NVA soldiers belonging to the 4th Infantry Regiment, who tried to advance to the walls to set satchel charges. A B-40 rocket round toppled him from his perch and allowed the attackers to storm the gate. Here they encountered some US Marines manning a bunker. They too slowed the attack until falling to a hail of RPG rounds. The time bravely bought allowed the defenders, including a tough crew of Australian warrant officers, to form a cohesive defence. The enemy changed tactics and tried to subdue the garrison with mortars and automatic weapons fire delivered from overlooking buildings. Isolated, unaware that enemy attacks had exploded nation wide, the garrison hunkered down and prayed for help.

All around their compound, and across the river, the 4th and 6th NVA Regiments and their VC comrades controlled most of the city and were freely roaming the streets. While the combat soldiers began fortifying mortar and machine-gun positions, special operatives began rounding up the people on their numerous lists. From atop the Citadel flagpole, a huge red-blue-gold Viet Cong flag flew. It had taken about two hours for the Communists to capture Hue, the country's second largest city.

Relief Force

Eight miles south of the city was the US Marine Corps Phu Bai Combat Base. Here the assistant commander of the 1st Marine Division, Brigadier General Foster LaHue, sifted through reports telling him of enemy activity throughout his area of responsibility. Included in the reports was one sent by the beleaguered defenders of the MACV compound, which had slowly drifted through the chain of command. Having been filtered by so many command levels, it conveyed little sense of urgency. Amid the confusion, LaHue apparently failed to appreciate both the scale and the critical nature of events in Hue. But, responding to orders, he did send reinforcements. Two and a half platoons belonging to 'A' Company, 1/1 Marines, boarded trucks and headed for Hue, not knowing that close to a full division of enemy soldiers awaited them.

Fortunately, the Marines married up with four M-48 Patton tanks along the way. As the small convoy neared Hue's outskirts, Communist marksmen opened fire and wounded several grunts. The convoy ran the gauntlet of fire, crossed a teetering canal bridge that enemy sappers had partially destroyed and approached a cluster of buildings. They reminded the company commander, Captain Gordon Batcheller, of an old western town, two-storey wooden buildings with no sidewalks, and – most ominously – with no people. The captain ordered his men out of the trucks and on to the tanks. Then, in best Marine Corps tradition, he boarded the lead tank and ordered the advance. From the tank decks the grunts sprayed the buildings with fire as they drove by. In return came a tremendous volume of AK-47 fire and volleys of RPGs. One RPG thudded into the leading tank spraying Batcheller with shrapnel and cutting the legs off his radioman. The survivors gathered along a ditch and tended their wounded. From adjacent buildings and rooftops Batcheller could see NVA infantrymen firing at his unit. It was very different from the paddy and jungle war where one seldom saw the enemy. Alpha Company needed help.

Around noon the commanders at Phu Bai learned of 'A' Company's plight. Lieutenant

Hue

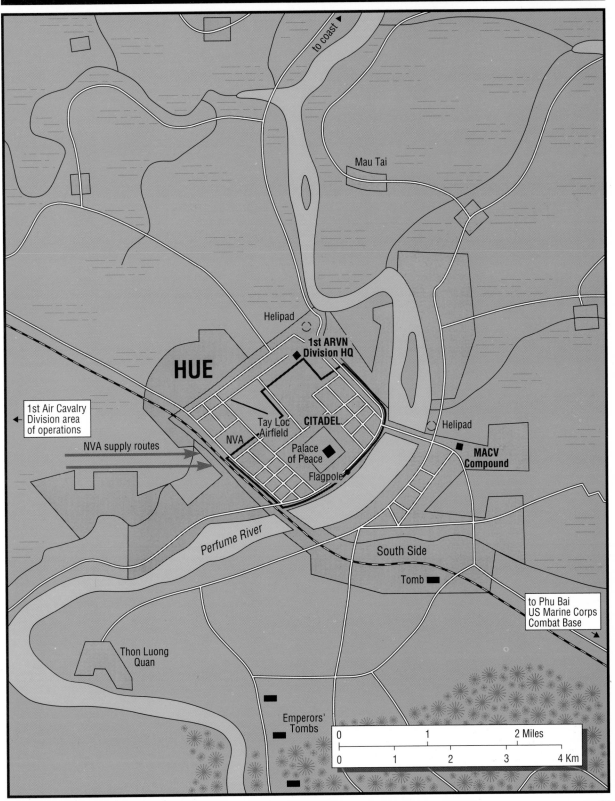

to coast ▶

Mau Tai

Helipad

HUE

1st ARVN Division HQ

1st Air Cavalry Division area of operations

Tay Loc Airfield

CITADEL

NVA

Helipad

Palace of Peace

MACV Compound

NVA supply routes

Flagpole

Perfume River

South Side

Tomb

to Phu Bai US Marine Corps Combat Base

Thon Luong Quan

Emperors' Tombs

0		1		2 Miles

0	1	2	3	4 Km

Joining the 'A' Company convoy were two Army 'Dusters', 40mm anti-aircraft weapons used with deadly effect against ground targets.

Marine Corps Patton tanks helped the grunts edge their way forward through Hue's streets. An officer recalls that the tanks drew heavy enemy fire: 'The moment a tank stuck its nose around the corner of a building, it looked like the Fourth of July' such was the volume and variety of hostile fire. One tank received 121 hits and went through five crews. Survivors came out looking 'like they were punch drunk'. This Patton halts before a destroyed canal bridge in Hue.

Colonel Marcus Gravel received the mission of taking another company, Golf 2/5, forward to retrace Alpha Company's steps and try to relieve them. He had no information other than Alpha Company was pinned down. Naked valour would have to substitute for preparation, firepower and tactics. Although the NVA would ambush, with dismal regularity, most of the convoys that drove along the road to Hue, this group made it without incident. They joined Alpha Company's survivors, now led by a wounded gunnery sergeant, and fought their way towards the MACV compound. A dug-in NVA machine-gun opened fire. Although already wounded, Sergeant Alfredo Gonzalez crawled towards it along a roadside ditch. Drawing near, he tossed a grenade into the position and silenced the machine-gun. The advance continued to the MACV compound. One of the defenders was to recall: 'I have little doubt that many of us would not be alive today, had those Marines not arrived.'

Once the objective had been attained, helicopters arrived to take out the many wounded. Then Gravel's two much-reduced companies received new orders from LaHue. He was to drive across the Perfume River, through the Citadel, and link up with General Truong in the 1st ARVN Division compound. Gravel protested to no avail. LaHue radioed back: 'Proceed.' Sadly, headquarters was out of touch with reality and would remain so for far too long. The misguided effort inevitably failed. The advance reached half way across the Perfume River bridge when NVA machine-gunners opened fire. Ten Marines fell dead or wounded in the opening volley. Golf Company pressed on, only to be ambushed in the narrow, winding streets bordering the Citadel. Gravel ordered an unauthorized retreat. Fifty of Golf's 150 men had been killed or wounded. That night, Gravel raged against the foolish orders that had sent his men to their doom. The only thing he felt thankful for was that the NVA had made a mistake too. Instead of holding fire just a little longer, which would have drawn Golf Company hopelessly into the maze of streets near the Citadel, they had shown their inexperience and fired too soon. The thought that the other side made mistakes provided some comfort as the two

Platoon Sergeant Alfredo Gonzalez, 21 years old, served with Alpha Company during its ambush on 31 January. When his unit suffered intense enemy fire, and although wounded from multiple shrapnel hits, Gonzalez rushed through the kill zone to rescue wounded Marines and drag them to shelter. Later in the action, he crawled along a roadside ditch to hand-grenade an enemy machine-gun that continued to pin his unit down. Four days later, having refused medical evacuation, while fighting through the Joan of Arc School, Gonzalez kicked in a door and led the rush into a school room. The NVA fired a hail of RPGs from point-blank range across the courtyard. The sergeant returned the fire with LAW rockets and silenced the enemy position. Suddenly a last enemy rocket entered the room striking Gonzalez in the midsection. Called 'the perfect Marine' by his officer, Gonzalez received a posthumous Medal of Honor for his conduct on 31 January.

depleted companies manned a defensive perimeter around the MACV compound on the South Side.

The successful defence of the MACV compound on the South Side, and the concurrent defence of the 1st ARVN Division HQ compound in the northern part of Hue unhinged Communist defensive plans. Helicopters could, and did, land reinforcements at these two points. Both then served as bases from which to begin the counter-attack to recapture the city. Instead of having a secure perimeter along fixed lines, the Communists had to defend against multiple threats including eruptions from within what they had thought would be their defensive perimeter. This was the significance of the gallant defence of the two strongpoints during the initial terror filled hours of the Tet Offensive. It also highlights the importance of the successful relief drive by the two Marine Corps companies during the first day.

Counter-Attack

One of the first Communist targets had been the jail, housing some 2,500 inmates. After liberation, about 500 of them joined the attacking forces. The attackers also captured numerous American-made weapons when they seized the ARVN armoury

A Marine observation plane makes a low-level pass over the Perfume River. Lieutenant Colonel Gravel's Marines successfully assaulted the river but could not expand their bridgehead on the far side.

during their opening assault. This, together with their ability to keep an open supply line from the A Shau valley, some 30 miles to the west, meant that the Communists were heavily armed and possessed ample ammunition. In addition, five reinforcing battalions joined the nine that made the initial assault. The weather too aided the Communists. Recurring misty drizzle greatly hampered Allied airpower. However, the rigid Communist plan could not adapt to the changed circumstances caused by the two Allied strong-points within their lines. Instead of making a major effort to eliminate these positions, the attackers yielded the initiative, dug-in and awaited the Allied counter-attack.

The second day in Hue, 1 February, established the pattern for the remainder of the battle. The generals, from LaHue on up, spoke in terms of 'mopping-up' and 'pushing the VC out of Hue this morning'. Meanwhile, three Marine companies, eventually reinforced by a fourth, began a building by building struggle through an eleven by nine block area to clear the South Side. Every alley, street corner, window, and garden wall harboured potential death. The only way to advance was to

M48A3 Patton tank of 1st Tank Battalion, USMC, Hue. Illustration by Peter Sarson and Tony Bryan.

After fighting up a street, through a garden and into a house against tough resistance, a Marine officer who had led the charge took time to inspect the enemy position. He found two-foot-thick concrete walls with bunker-style firing slits. The slits provided a perfect field of fire down the street and into the building from where the Marines had staged the assault. Stepping back, the officer could only mutter: 'Son of a bitch, son of a bitch.'

blast an entrance with bazooka or recoilless rifle fire and then send fireteams and squads into the breach. To charge through a blow-in door, clamber over an exposed garden wall, or sprint across an intersection required great bravery. The Marines' special *esprit de corps* motivated the 18- and 19-year-old grunts to do these things and more, repeatedly, for nearly a month.

In times past, a wounded Marine expected to receive medical evacuation and an extended recovery period. In Hue, those suffering from any but the most disabling wounds commonly were patched up by medical personnel and voluntarily returned to duty. A company leader later wrote: 'I had several men who had shrapnel in legs and arms and hobbled around and begged me not to medevac them.' Another officer thought that 'it was payback time' for the Marines who had endured prior months of sniper fire and booby traps without being able to hit back. The presence of every rifle-wielding grunt was badly needed. Since the High Command seriously underestimated their opposition, the attackers received paltry reinforcements. For most of the long battle, a mere two understrength battalions conducted the

advance. A frustrated battalion commander wondered: 'Why must they always piecemeal us into battle?'

While the Marines operated on the South Side, Lieutenant General Hoang Xuam Lam worked to recapture the Citadel. He planned to use the 1st ARVN Division HQ's perimeter as a base of operations. First he needed to send reinforcements, and this proved very hard. The 7th ARVN Armored Cavalry and two airborne battalions had to force a convoy through a major ambush to reach Hue. Similarly, two battalions of the 1st ARVN Division's 3rd Regiment took fearful losses during their approach march. During 1 February, the 2nd ARVN Airborne Battalions and the 7th ARVN Cavalry recaptured Tay Loc Airfield, but only after suffering heavy losses including twelve armoured vehicles and the death of the cavalry squadron commander. Facing resistance every bit as tough as that confronting the American Marines across the river, the South Vietnamese slowly advanced through well-prepared fortified positions. By 4 February, a battalion of the 3rd ARVN Regiment – a regiment that would consistently fight harder than any other

Flak-vested 1st Regiment Marines move a 106mm recoilless rifle into position to open the way through the next block of buildings during the house-to-house fighting in Hue.

The Americans tended to denigrate the combat skills and bravery of their South Vietnamese allies. After-combat reports and subsequent history focused on actions featuring Americans. However, ARVN forces took the brunt of the Tet Offensive and their losses reflected this. In Saigon alone, while the American attention focused on the Embassy, racetrack and Tan Son Nhut, on the first day of battle 88 ARVN soldiers died and 239 were wounded. The élite Airborne, Ranger and Marine units suffered most of these losses. *ARVN Airborne soldiers with a captured Viet Cong.* In Hue the American Marines felt badly let down by the lack of contribution from the ARVN. Said one: 'The ARVN were an unruly lot and they made sure to stay far to the rear of the advancing Marines . . . We'd see them after a pitched battle, driving up in trucks to loot the buildings we had just captured . . . I think if the ARVN ever enjoyed any fighting reputation with the Marines, they lost it in Hue.'

STREET FIGHTING IN HUE

1–27 February 1968. Typical urban combat scene as US and ARVN forces battle with NVA and VC units for control of the city.

The battle for the old Imperial Capital of Hue began on 31 January and continued until 2 March 1968. In a guerrilla war, Hue was an exception, an extended urban combat against a foe who tried to hold fixed objectives. The battle featured two NVA regiments backed by two VC sapper battalions against eight US and thirteen ARVN infantry battalions. The urban landscape denied the Allies their two greatest weapons – mobility and firepower. The battle became a savage small-unit house-to-house combat. After the first few days, the ARVN units had spent their impetus. It was left to the Marines to recapture Hue.

Aided by local sympathizers and impressed civilian labour, the defenders turned each block into a fortress. They sited crew-served weapons at doorways and windows to sweep the streets; they used back alleys and lanes to hasten reinforcements to threatened sectors and to launch sudden, unexpected counter-attacks.

Marine scout-sniper team

NVA counter-attack force guided by locals infiltrating Marines' positions

Reserve fire team pinned down

Stretcher team trying to reach wounded

106mm recoilless rifle for direct-fire support

For the attackers it was a battle of fire-team rushes. Battle-scarred Patton tanks operated in the main street, but in these confined areas they were unmistakable targets for NVA machine-guns and RPGs. Holed repeatedly, the tanks would withdraw briefly. The dead and wounded crew were removed, replacement crews installed and the tanks returned to combat. Many tanks went through several crews a day.

Behind them came the flak-vested grunts. Working in close co-ordination with the tanks, they methodically reduced the Communist positions and clawed their way forward.

From adjacent buildings, Marine scout-sniper teams tried to eliminate Communist snipers while providing covering fire for the grunts in the street. Deadly man-to-man sniper duels ensued.

Jeep-mounted recoilless rifles and Ontos anti-tank vehicles gave direct-fire support. Lightly armoured, they utilized bold hit-and-run tactics. They would appear suddenly around a debris-clogged corner, fire, and then dash for cover.

NVA snipers

Bunker with machine-gun
and anti-tank rockets

Day's objective
Fortified church tower blocking
advance towards citadel

Fortified buildings with
crew-served weapons

NVA reserves

CS tear-gas to
cover assault

Bazooka
team

Assault group

Tank/infantry
team

When assault up
the main streets proved
impossible, Marine fire-
teams manoeuvered
through back alleys to
attack from the rear.

Numerous garden walls
and hedgerows made such
tactics difficult. To work
up courage for the assault,

CONTINUED OVERLEAF

CONTINUED FROM OVERLEAF:

many Marine teams chanted in unison as they awaited the signal to charge. A bazooka round provided this signal when it blasted a hole in the masonry wall separating one garden from another. Then the assault teams rushed through the breach. Too often the first through the breach fell to the defender's withering automatic weapons fire.

Both sides utilized CS tear gas rounds. Thus the battle was one of the few of the war where the presence of gas forced the combatants to fight wearing gas masks. Hue was urban combat at its worst. A day's advance was measured in yards.

ARVN formation and take crippling losses as a result – stormed the An Hoa gate taking the Citadel's north-west wall. This effort consumed the aggressive spirit of the airborne and regular ARVN forces. On the night of 6 February, a ferocious nocturnal NVA counter-attack by storm troops using grappling hooks drove the ARVN forces from the recently recaptured south-west wall.

The First Team

Meanwhile, outside Hue, a battalion of the hard-fighting 1st Air Cavalry Division air-assaulted into the middle of the Communist supply line in an effort to interdict the flow of supplies to Hue. Attacking through the fog, 2/12 Cav had to do without its customary helicopter gunship and aerial rocket artillery support. Confronted with two dug-in NVA battalions, the cavalry failed and retired to prepare against the expected counter-attacks.

At dawn a heavy mortar barrage landed within the 150-yard-wide battalion perimeter. Charging NVA infantry, firing their AK-47s from the hip and supported by numerous machine-guns giving grazing support fire, followed the bombardment with repeated assaults. Only accurate defensive fire from a 105mm battery preserved the position.

As the afternoon wore on, casualties mounted as mortar rounds scored direct hits within the crowded perimeter. The cavalry's ammunition ran low. Medevac helicopters were able to rescue only the most seriously wounded in the face of heavy Communist fire. As nightfall approached, the battalion commander, Lieutenant Colonel Dick Sweet, realized that his isolated unit could not hold out. Sweet made a bold decision. Rather than await the final NVA assault, his unit would break out from their perimeter. Furthermore, instead of heading in the expected direction toward the nearest friendly unit, the cavalry set out across an exposed rice paddy. The most reliable point man led the way. As Private Hector Comacho recalls: 'It was dark, but I trusted myself. The hardest part was finding some place where everyone could go, and making sure that everyone could keep up.' Officers instructed the troopers not to fire under any circumstances, and if they received fire they were to hit the ground and remain silent. Sweet recalls the march: 'We had men who had refused to be medevaced that afternoon. They hid their wounds so they could stay with the battalion . . . You'd see them limping; there was no talk. No noise at all. I've never seen such discipline in a unit . . . You'd find that the man up ahead of you who was dragging a foot had a bullet in his leg, and had

Prohibitions on the use of artillery, such as the very accurate 8-inch howitzer, made the recapture of Hue even more difficult. The Allies had to retake Hue one building at a time.

A Patton tank supports the 1/5 Marines beside the citadel walls on 12 February.

Eventually the Air Cav was able to isolate Hue from outside reinforcements. Some 6,000 defenders held Hue for nearly a month. When it was all over, American commanders speculated what would have happened had the enemy sent one of the big 10,000-man divisions stationed along the DMZ into Hue. Westmoreland's replacement, Lieutenant General Creighton Abrams, thought he knew. In 1969 he told a reporter: 'We'd still be fighting there.'

it there for almost 24 hours. That's why the night march worked.'

Taking all their wounded with them, the troopers trudged through a rainy, cold, pitch-black night. After a perilous eleven-hour march, 2/12 Cav arrived atop a low hill from where they could receive helicopter resupply. It had been exceedingly well done, but still the cavalry had failed to shut off the Communist flow of supplies into Hue.

House-to-House Combat

Back in the city, the difficult house-to-house fighting frustrated the Allied commanders. Prohibitions on the use of artillery and air strikes, intended to preserve historic sites within Hue, coupled with poor weather limited Allied progress. On 9 February, a reporter asked the commander of the 1st ARVN Division whether the Imperial Palace, which served as a defensive strongpoint, was not too important to bomb. General Truong pragmatically replied: 'You exaggerate. It is good for tourists, but if we meet heavy resistance we will use air strikes, artillery, everything.'

Still, the poor weather and the special Rules of Engagement employed in Hue meant that the Marines went without their customary fire support. Fortunately the big Patton tanks and the 106mm recoilless rifles provided accurate direct-fire weapons to reduce a sniper's lair or a machine-gun nest. First though, these positions had to be located, and this was usually done at cost. A Marine recalls watching a decimated platoon huddle beneath one of the ubiquitous garden walls. Several boosted one grunt over the wall. As his head reached the top a concealed AK-47 fired. The grunt flopped to the ground. He had been shot in the face. Crying out 'Momma!', he died.

By 10 February the Marines had cleared the South Side. Now they had to turn their attention to the Citadel across the river. Higher command back at Phu Bai remained badly out of touch with reality. For example, its plan called for crossing a bridge that had been destroyed by NVA sappers one week earlier. Although ARVN forces had cleared about three-quarters of the Citadel, the NVA still held formidable positions and retained a functioning supply line to their strongholds in the western mountains. In addition they struck back with bold counter-attacks whenever possible. Indicative of their fighting spirit was a spectacular nocturnal raid by VC combat-swimmers, who mined another important river bridge and dropped two of its spans into the water.

Reinforcements arrived for the drive against the Citadel. Vietnamese Marines, having just finished clearing Saigon of VC resistance, arrived to relieve the battered airborne battalions. The US 1/5 Marines entered battle on 12 February. The street fighting chewed the battalion up as witnessed by its losses among platoon leaders. After nine days of combat, its ten rifle platoons, which would normally be led by first lieutenants, were commanded by three second lieutenants, one gunnery sergeant, two staff sergeants, two buck sergeants, and two senior corporals.

On 26 February, soldiers moving through the Gia Hoi High School yard came across freshly turned earth. They investigated and uncovered the bound bodies of numerous civilians. They were the first of a colossal number of victims of a Communist atrocity, the dimensions of which were not fully appreciated until mid-1970 when the last graves were found. Around Hue, searchers eventually found 2,810 bodies, while nearly 2,000 more remained missing. Apparently the slaughter began when the VC first occupied Hue. Special commandos had rounded up and executed civilians on a blacklist of government workers and politicians. When it appeared that the Communists might be able to hold Hue, a second wave of executions took place. This time the victims were intellectuals and students who seemed to represent a threat to the new Communist order. When it became clear that the battle was going adversely, the largest number of killings occurred. The VC systematically killed anyone who might be able to identify the local Communists who had surfaced during the offensive. Following the mass killings, they tried to hide their work. Preoccupied by the ongoing combat the Allies failed to publicize the atrocity. The Press tended to disbelieve the early reports of mass graves, since these came from sources they considered discredited. Instead reporters concentrated on stories of Allied setbacks and pictures of the urban destruction.

The exhaustion of this Marine is apparent as he sleeps on the deck of an Ontos, an anti-tank vehicle used for direct fire support and armed with six 106mm recoilless rifles.

M50A1 Ontos of 3rd Anti-Tank Battalion, US Marine Corps. Illustration by Peter Sarson and Tony Bryan.

The difficulty of the first assaults against the Citadel equalled anything in Marine Corps history. Tanks could barely manage to operate in the narrow alleys near the Citadel's high walls and towers. Wide scale use of debilitating CS gas helped, but a day's advance frequently did not exceed 200 yards. The Marines paid in blood for most of these gains. During the week of 13-20 February, four Marine companies suffered 47 killed, 240 seriously wounded, and another 60 wounded who remained in combat. Casualties were so high that the Marines sent replacements directly from their instructional camps in the United States. Hopelessly maladroit for the complex city fighting, they died far too often. Yet the relentless advance by the flak-vested grunts forced the defenders to face the inevitable. On 16 February, radio intercept technicians decoded a message from the NVA commander inside Hue. It spoke of heavy losses, including the senior officer, and requested permission to withdraw. Communist HQ sent the reply to remain and fight.

By 21 February the Allies could see the end. The 1st Cavalry had managed to close the enemy supply lines into Hue. By the following day the US Marines could prepare for a final push and reported lighter enemy contact than on any previous day. Similarly, ARVN forces resumed the advance. By order of the high command, the Marines allowed the 1st ARVN Division's Black Panther Company – a unit that had fought long and hard, an exception, most Marines thought – to make the final assault. The Black Panthers charged right at the Imperial Palace, yelling and firing as they advanced, some carrying scaling ladders to get over the walls. NVA resistance had collapsed. The ARVN soldiers hauled down the Viet Cong flag that had flown for 25 days. Unaware of the ARVN contribution at Hue, a Marine officer bitterly observed: 'The MACV records will reflect that the ARVN . . . took the Citadel. That was strictly public relations hogwash . . . The 1st Battalion, 5th Marines, took the Citadel. The ARVN were spectators.'

Hue was the longest sustained infantry battle the war had so far seen. By Vietnam standards, losses had been high. During 26 days of combat ARVN units lost 384 killed and more than 1,800 wounded; US Army casualties were 74 dead and 507 wounded; the three Marine battalions, 142 and 857, respectively. The Allies claimed to have killed over 5,000 and captured 89. Civilian losses, both victims of Communist atrocity and hapless targets caught in the urban crossfire, amounted to some 5,800 killed. Much of the once-beautiful city of Hue lay in rubble.

Grunts belonging to 'A' Company, 1/1 Marines, leave a recaptured church on 9 February.

ASSESSMENT

During the preceding 25 years, the American military had made a habit of playing the victim for enemy surprise attacks. Pearl Harbor, Kasserine Pass, the Battle of the Bulge and the Chinese intervention along the Yalu River had all caught the Americans unawares. The synchronized violence of the Tet Offensive was matched perhaps only by the Germans' Ardennes Offensive. Of all these surprise attacks, only the Tet Offensive achieved decisive results.

Yet, by conventional military calculation, Tet was an enormous Allied success. At a cost of some 4,000 Americans killed and wounded and between 4,000 and 8,000 ARVN soldiers killed, the Communists suffered 40,000 to 50,000 battlefield deaths. Most importantly, large numbers of irreplaceable local Viet Cong fighters and cadres had died. Simply put, the enemy had concentrated, and his masses had been consumed by American firepower. This battlefield success has been obscured by the more important political consequences of the Tet Offensive. However, Tet was part of an unbroken record forged by the American soldier from 1965 to 1973 of not losing a single important battle. As Douglas Pike, one of the few experts to study and comprehend the Viet Cong and North Vietnamese, notes: 'Had the Vietnam War been another conventional war, had it been decided on the basis of past wars, it would have been over by mid-1968 with the defeat of the Communist forces.' Indeed, the way the public perceived the battle astonished many American veterans. Standing next to enemy corpses stacked like cordwood outside his unit's headquarters, a cavalry officer wondered how: 'To our complete bewilderment in the weeks that followed, nobody ever publicized this feat of battlefield triumph. Instead, we read that we had been defeated!'

It is also important to remember that the Communist strategists had designed the offensive

President Nguyen Van Thieu places a commemorative plaque for the victims of the Hue massacre in 1971.

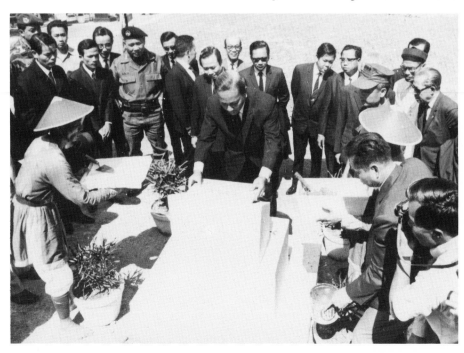

to impress the South Vietnamese rather than the American public. A top North Vietnamese General, Tran Do, commented after the war:

'We didn't achieve our main objective, which was to spur uprisings throughout the south. Still, we inflicted heavy casualties . . . As for making an impact in the United States, it had not been our intention – but it turned out to be a fortunate result.'

In many ways the embassy battle was a microcosm of the entire war. The weapons and explosives used during the attack easily slipped past the hopelessly inadequate South Vietnamese security cordon around the capital. The guerrillas mustered in a building owned by a female Viet Cong agent of thirteen years' standing who had been arrested several times for subversive activities. Yet her building was not under surveillance. The attackers received help from an embassy driver, whom the Americans had often jokingly said 'must be a VC' because he was so smart. They drove past South Vietnamese police who ran rather than sound the alarm. In the attack the VC hardly proved supermen. They were inadequately briefed, opened fire too soon, and showed no initiative once their leaders fell.

Interestingly enough, the Communist high command had not appreciated the potential psychological impact of the embassy assault. It was just one, rather minor, target among many. In fact, the general who commanded the Saigon offensives criticized the embassy attack several days after it took place. He believed it had been poorly conceived. Only when they understood the attack's

impact on the American public did the Communists begin to propagandize it. Here was the paradox of the war: a small, ill-conceived, tactically flawed attack against an insignificant military objective, designed to impress the South Vietnamese, proved the decisive action of the war because of its impact on the American public.

Communist planners had timed the offensive for a holiday period when the South Vietnamese and Americans would be less vigilant. Conveniently, it was also at a critical time in the United States. It was just before the first presidential primaries and thus, in the words of Don Oberdorfer, 'caught the American political system at its moment of greatest irresolution and potential for change'. Incomplete, inaccurate, and biased Press coverage of the combat influenced the public's

perception. However, even if this type of coverage were discounted, the public recognized by the widespread and ferocious nature of the Tet Offensive that the enemy remained much stronger than their politicians and generals had led them to believe. The choice seemed to be to escalate yet again or to seek terms.

The first option seemed unpromising because strategically the Tet Offensive undercut Westmoreland's attrition strategy. The essential weakness of this strategy should have been apparent before Tet. In mid-1967 the NVA comprised some 450,000 men of whom a mere 70,000 served in Laos and South Vietnam. Each year about

The 'Mini Tet' Offensive in May brought a return to street fighting in Saigon.

200,000 young men reached the age of eighteen. Simple arithmetic could show that the Communists had the manpower to endure the kind of terrible losses they suffered in 1967 for years to come. If attrition strategy could not kill the enemy fast enough, in spite of amazing favourable kill ratios of 10 to 1 or better, then the outcome hinged on will. Recent history against the French, let alone the long history of Vietnamese resistance to the Chinese, clearly demonstrated that Communist morale, which had assumed the mantle of stubborn Vietnamese nationalism, would not crack.

If escalation would not work, negotiation seemed the only alternative. Many historians point to the night of 27 February 1968 as a turning point in the war. That evening, the popular and much-respected American broadcaster Walter Cronkite delivered a televised special report summing up the Tet Offensive. Cronkite had just returned from a whirlwind tour of South Vietnam and what he had seen had greatly depressed him. He began his report in the most despairing manner. While the camera panned over battle damage in Saigon, he intoned that the ruins 'in this burned and blasted and weary land . . . mean success or setback, victory or defeat, depending on who you talk to'. He proceeded to juxtapose official comments minimizing setbacks with selected eyewitness accounts that claimed disaster. He left no doubt what he personally felt, using such terms as 'the shattered pieces' of pacification, stating that the South Vietnamese government 'could salvage a measure of victory from defeat'. His interviews and film seemed to discredit all official pronouncements. Cronkite concluded:

'We have been too often disappointed by the optimism of the American leaders . . . To say that we are closer to victory today is to believe, in the face of the evidence, the optimists who have been wrong in the past . . . To say that we are mired in stalemate seems the only realistic, yet unsatisfactory, conclusion . . . it is increasingly clear to this reporter that the only rational way out will be to negotiate, not as victors, but as an honorable people who lived up to their pledge to defend democracy, and did the best they could.'

Initially, Press reports including Cronkite's did little to alter the public's attitude toward the war.

Whereas before Tet 45 per cent believed that sending American troops to Vietnam was a mistake, 49 per cent felt this way after Tet. More important, the extremely influential Eastern television and print media moguls, and substantial numbers of the Washington, DC, opinion makers and politicians, concluded that the war was lost. They began to disseminate this message to the country, and the public listened. Consequently, February and March led to a turning point in American opinion about the war. During the two months following Tet, one in every five Americans switched from pro- to anti-war. Johnson's popularity among both pro- and anti-war people plummeted. Public frustration encompassed roughly equal numbers of hawks – who were angered at the administration's half-measures that seemed only to produce more dead American boys – and the doves who simply wanted to get out.

The American Press played a decisive role in the Tet Offensive. Yet, in both detail, analysis and conclusion, Press reporting of the Tet Offensive was highly misleading. An inexperienced, or lazy, reporter covering the war from the comfort of Saigon could not understand how the Communists had been able to mass for their surprise assaults without detection. They reported that it must be because of a sympathetic civilian population who helped conceal Communist movements. Here was more evidence, ran a common Press refrain, to undermine the administration's claims about the war's progress.

In fact, the majority of the South Vietnamese civilian population was neutral, more interested in survival than anything else. The Communists needed little assistance beyond that provided by their local cadres, who represented a small percentage of the total population. The terrain provided the rest. Even Saigon lay surrounded by swamps, woods and canals. The Communists took advantage of this concealment to march in secret to staging areas on the city's outskirts. But this important fact was unknown to the majority of the Press and so remained unreported to the public. The public could only conclude that an obliging citizenry had escorted the enemy to the gates of the American bases. Similarly, the Press had few contacts within the South Vietnamese military.

The handful of reports that did focus on ARVN performance highlighted those units and leaders who had fought the poorest. This message reinforced the growing sense that America fought alone.

At the time, political and military leaders from Johnson and Westmoreland down blamed the Press for losing the war. The effort continued for years thereafter as discredited leaders sought to recover prestige. But their carping obscures the fact already described that even with a fully muzzled Press America had no viable war-winning strategy.

By the end of March the domestic sea change led to the announcement by the proud, enbittered President Lyndon Johnson that he would not run for re-election. In an effort at negotiated settlement, Americans and North Vietnamese met in Paris in mid-May 1968, some three months after Tet. American leaders never fully comprehended the masterful Communist negotiating strategy of 'fighting and talking'. More Americans would be killed after the 'peace talks' opened then before they began.

On 3 July, General William Westmoreland departed as MACV commander to become the new Army Chief of Staff. Few doubted that, defeated and discredited, he had been kicked upstairs. Responding to domestic political pressure, his replacement – General Creighton Abrams – ordered sweeping strategic changes. American tactical aggressiveness gave way to the new mandate to reduce American battlefield casualties. Equally important, the high command decided that, henceforth, South Vietnamese troops would switch from pacification to mainstream combat. This decision, formally announced by the Joint Chiefs of Staff on 16 April 1968, marked the beginning of what would become the ill-fated 'Vietnamization' policy. Thus the Tet Offensive achieved a certain symmetry of results: it destroyed the Viet Cong but caused the Americans to begin to disengage as they turned the war over to the South Vietnamese. The future would depend on

Scenes of urban death and destruction once again provided film for television cameras.

Vietnamese Rangers collect the bodies of slain Viet Cong in June 1968.

the contest between the regulars of North and South Vietnam.

Meanwhile, in selected areas American soldiers would continue offensive operations. But the nature of the war changed. Abrams, much to the disgust of more junior, hard-charging officers, responded to new political realities by emphasizing city security. He badly wanted to avoid a repeat of the Saigon and Hue battles. The need to defend cities took manpower away from offensive action. None the less, adequate ARVN-US planning for Saigon's defence did not take place until after the second major Communist assault exploded through the capital in May.

The Tet Offensive demonstrated to many the essential dilemma the American military faced in Vietnam: 'Guerrillas win if they don't lose. A standard army loses if it does not win.' Even this comment obscures the most important facet of the war: first and foremost it was a political struggle. The Communists clearly recognized this from the beginning and wove an integrated miltary/political war-winning strategy. American politicians refused to mobilize the political will of the country, meddled with military strategy to its profound detriment but, in the end, listened to the generals who claimed they could conquer on the battlefield. The military, in turn, did not appreciate the political consequences of what it did. They had some understanding of domestic American consequences, but little regard for the impact of operations on the citizens of Vietnam. A North Vietnamese officer, explaining why America lost, put it most plainly: 'Your second weak point was to try to win the hearts and minds of the people while you were using bombs to kill them.'

During the Tet Offensive the American military had achieved notable successes and suffered some important failures. In spite of advance warning, Westmoreland had failed to alert adequately all units before the enemy assault. He was caught in mid-shift of major formations northward. He underestimated the psychological importance of Saigon and Hue. He failed to establish a co-ordinated ARVN-US plan for city defence.

Tactically, the surprise offensive caught the Allies short of weapons and lacking appropriate tactics for urban warfare. The military had con-

sciously discarded many of the heavier weapons associated with conventional combat in order to improve mobility in Vietnam's hinterland. Suddenly forced into tough house-to-house fighting, soldiers found themselves without direct-fire heavy weapons such as the Marine's 106mm recoilless rifle. They had to rely upon helicopter gunships, air strikes and artillery, all of which were less accurate and increased destruction of civilian life and property.

Tet was a major setback for the slowly improving South Vietnamese military. Along with their advisers, ARVN units fought unaided on the ground in 36 of 44 provincial capitals, 64 of 242 district capitals, and 50 hamlets attacked at the beginning of Tet. The best units acquitted themselves very well during the fighting. Some poorly regarded divisions fought much better then expected. Others, such as the 2nd Division at Quang Ngai which had been judged combat effective, displayed little fighting spirit. Overall, the units that fought the best suffered serious losses and declined as a result of Tet. The official casualty count probably understated South Vietnamese losses: 4,954 killed, 15,097 wounded, 926 missing. Unofficial estimates counted at least double this total of soldiers killed.

The stunning violence of the Communist assault demonstrated to South Vietnamese civilians that their own government, supported by the Americans and despite their weapons and promises, could not protect them. The Communist occupation of the old Imperial City of Hue had an adverse impact on South Vietnamese morale comparable to the American public's reaction to the embassay attack. Nation-wide war-weariness set in and desertion rates soared. At the end of 1967 the desertion rate was 10.5 per thousand. After heavy fighting and new mobilization orders, the July 1968 rate was 16.5 per thousand. Some 13,506 men deserted in July alone.

The Tet Offensive was also a bad setback for the pacification effort. More than one-third of the ARVN regular battalions assigned to pacification in rural areas had to withdraw into nearby cities. In the absence of protection, half the rural development teams, who had been making some progress at winning popular support for the government, abandoned their villages. These teams were the lynchpin of the pacification effort, which, in turn, was fundamental to Allied strategy.

From the Communist perspective, on the battlefield Tet had achieved far less than had been hoped. The Hanoi command had seemingly over-estimated the readiness of the southern people to rise and overthrow the government. Giap had apparently yielded to impatience and misjudged the situation. The months following the offensive witnessed a doctrinarial debate within the Hanoi Command. A key conclusion was that victory could be achieved by remaining in Mao's Stage Two of guerrilla war without ever massing for Stage Three combat. This conclusion was a dramatic departure from previous doctrine.

The war would now be won by the 'super-guerrilla'. This fighter was anything but the black-pyjama-clad, lightly armed, local guerrilla. Rather he was a well-trained fighting man armed with the best weapons that the Communist world could provide. He used modern communications equip-ment to co-ordinate his effort, and would conduct deadly raids against enemy installations in order to limit the enemy's initiative and wear him down. Doctrine aside, however, such were the Tet losses that the Communists were unable to launch any major attacks during 1969.

The Tet Offensive, along with the subsequent summer offensives, nearly annihilated the Viet Cong. The VC suffered irreplaceable losses among key leaders and agents. As one survivor lamented: 'We lost our best people.' Henceforth, the North Vietnamese would have to bear the brunt of all combat operations. Combined VC/NVA casualties had been so severe that they required four years to recover before launching another major offensive. Even then, the Easter offensive of 1972 relied upon NVA soldiers for 90 per cent of the combat.

Given the important differences between Hanoi's and the National Liberation Front's objectives, the destruction of the Viet Cong was not entirely unwelcome in the North. The Offen-sive killed off many leaders who might have challenged Northern hegemony. Events after the war support this dark view of Hanoi's strategy. Many surviving high-ranking Viet Cong were terribly disheartened at what befell their move-ment. They felt betrayed by their northern brothers. Some had to flee the county. Northern historians, on the other hand, minimized the importance of the VC's contribution. Some vir-tually denied that the NLF and the VC had much to do with the war. While as of 1989, Hanoi has apparently solid control over the country, accord-ing to reports from people who flee the country, strife between north and south still simmers beneath the surface. From the Viet Cong perspec-tive, Tet must be seen as a terrible bloodbath, a catastrophic defeat.

For the North Vietnamese, Tet marked the turn of the tide. But this was not readily appre-ciated at the time. Responding to a question of whether the High Command knew they had won the war in 1968, a general replied: 'Yes and no. Nixon began the withdrawal, but Vietnamization was a difficult period for us . . . 1969 and 1970 were very hard on us. The fighting was very fierce.'

While Communist post-mortems of many of the attacks, particularly those in Saigon, were full of honest self-criticizm, Hue was deemed a battle whose 'most outstanding feature was that we won an overall success'. The Communist command was particularly pleased to note that 'Hue was the place where reactionary spirit had existed for over ten years. However, it took us only a short time to drain it to its root.' Without apologies, such was the Viet Cong view of civilian massacre.

Whether the Communists could have endured an Allied counter-offensive during 1968 of the type proposed by Westmoreland is one of the tantalizing 'what ifs' of the Vietnam War. But as memories of the war's horror fade with time, and generals propound theories on how it could have been won, recall the words of a North Vietnamese officer who acknowledged the terrible losses suf-fered during Tet: 'We had hundreds of thousands killed in this war. We would have sacrificed one or two million more if necessary.'

The Tet Offensive of 1968 failed to defeat the American combat soldier on the battlefield, but it had defeated his general's strategy, his political leaders, and reversed the support of the people back home. It was one of the few battles of history that can be called decisive.

CHRONOLOGY

1967

7 July Decision in Hanoi to launch the General Offensive/General Uprising.
Late July Viet Cong leaders meet in Cambodia to plan how to implement the offensive.
29 July Detroit Riots, 15,339 federal and national guard troops sent to Detroit.
7 August Army Chief of Staff reports 'smell of success' surrounds Allied effort; beginning of Johnson administration propaganda campaign.
21-3 October Pentagon Riots; three battalions backed by tear gas repulse civilian stone- and bottle-throwing assault.
21 November General Westmoreland predicts US troop withdrawals to start in two years.
15 December Responsibility for Saigon's defence passes to ARVN.
20 December Westmoreland warns Washington of Communists' decision to attempt country-wide war-winning offensive.

1968

10 January Westmoreland orders US pullback to positions closer to Saigon.
20 January Siege of Khe Sanh begins.
23 January North Korea seizes USS *Pueblo*.
29 January Tet holiday ceasefire begins for Allies.
30 January Communists launch premature attack in I and II Corps areas.
31 January Nation-wide Communist offensive begins.
8 February NVA tanks overrun Lang Vei, outside Khe Sanh. Elsewhere, VC/NVA hold only Saigon suburbs and Hue citadel.
13 February Gallup poll reports 50 per cent disapprove of Johnson's handling of the war.
17 February Record weekly total of US casualties set during preceding seven days; 543 killed, 2,547 wounded.
18 February 45 cities and bases shelled but only four ground attacks.
21 February COSVN orders a pullback and return to harassing tactics.
24 February Hue's Imperial Palace recaptured.
27 February CBS's Walter Cronkite tells nation that negotiation is the only way out of the war.
1 March US Secretary of Defense Robert McNamara replaced.
10 March *New York Times* reports Westmoreland wants another 206,000 men.
12 March Eugene McCarthy wins 42 per cent of vote in New Hampshire Democratic primary election.
16-20 March Gallup poll finds more doves than hawks for first time.
20 March NVA pressure against Khe Sanh diminishes.
22 March Johnson announces Westmoreland will become Army Chief of Staff in mid-1968.
26 March Johnson's special advisers report country has lost confidence in war and that US should disengage.
31 March President Johnson announces partial bombing pause, willingness to negotiate and decision not to run for re-election.
16 April Pentagon announces a gradual policy change to return ARVN forces to the forefront of combat, the origin of 'Vietnamization'.
3 July Westmoreland replaced by Abrams.

1969

8 June First US troop withdrawal announced.

1972

30 March Communists launch first nation-wide

A GUIDE TO FURTHER READING

offensive since 1968. Much hard fighting. Backed by US airpower, ARVN wins out.

1973

29 March Last US troops withdraw.

1975

30 April NVA tanks spearhead capture of Saigon. South Vietnam surrenders.

1982

11 November Vietnam veterans memorial opens, healing the still-divisive scar of war.

BRAESTRUP, P. *Big Story*, Boulder, Colorado, 1977. A superb, 2-volume study of how the American media reprinted and interpreted Tet. Essential for understanding how the Communists achieved their success.

LUONG, Colonel H. *The General Offensives of 1968–69*, Washington, 1981. Sponsored by the US Army Center of Military History, it provides the South Vietnamese view of events. Candid analysis of the intelligence failure.

KARNOW, S. *Vietnam: A History*, New York, 1983. The best general history of America's Vietnam experience.

KELLEN, K. *Conversations with Enemy Soldiers in Late 1968/Early 1969: A Study of Motivation and Morale*, 1970. A penetrating report by the RAND Corporation containing interviews with captured enemy soldier.

NOLAN, K. *Battle for Hue Tet 1968*, New York, 1983. A grunt's-eye view of Vietnam's longest single battle.

OBERDORFER, D. *Tet!*, Garden City, NY, 1971. Somewhat unbalanced because of its publication date, a good broad-brushed account. Particularly good on the American domestic scene.

SON, Lieutenant-Colonel P. (senior editor). *The Viet Cong Tet Offensive 1968*, Saigon, 1969. The official South Vietnamese history. Lacks perspective given the publication date and political climate, but provides invaluable detail about ARVN operations.

STANTON, S. *The Rise and Fall of an American Army*, Novato, Ca, 1985. While biased with a very pro-military viewpoint, it is *the* 1-volume account of American military operations.

WARGAMING THE TET OFFENSIVE

For wargame purposes we may consider the three phases of the Tet Offensive: 1, the diversionary siege of Khe Sanh; 2, the surprise assaults; 3, the responses. In all three phases the end-game is important to both sides. The NVA/VC must attempt to recover as many bodies and weapons as possible, whereas the Americans and ARVN must rescue and evacuate their casualties.

The charts and campaign rules set out below are not designed for any specific set of rules and should be compatible with most commercially and privately produced sets. Nor are they to be seen as unalterable. In some circumstances, where research or scenario constraints dictate, they will need some minor alterations.

Khe Sanh combat base was besieged prior to the Tet Offensive. It may well have been a diversion to draw reserves away from the real objectives. The siege became mainly an air and artillery battle punctuated by several major NVA ground attacks. The defenders sent several patrols outside the base perimeter.

The Tet assaults did not come as a complete surprise everywhere. Intelligence had shown a large NVA build up in late 1967. However, the sheer scale of the offensive did come as a shock. Most, but not all, of the South Vietnamese units were at between 25 and 50 per cent of their effective strength through personnel being granted leave during the truce period. Thus the initial assaults met with varied resistance depending on the strength and state of alertness of the defenders. Since most targets in the initial stages of this offensive fell on the ARVN-held areas, some special rules are helpful for wargamers attempting realism in their scenarios. A dicing system can be used to determine the average strength of ARVN units. Note that the designation 'D10' is used for a die numbered 1 to 10 (some are numbered 0 to 9, in which case treat the 0 as 10). These dice are also

called percentage dice and are the only type to be used in these rules.

Table 1: AVRN strength

Strength of unit	D10 roll
30 per cent	1
40 per cent	2–3
50 per cent	4–5
60 per cent	7–8
70 per cent	9
75 per cent	10

A morale dicing system for units can also be used:

Table 2: Morale

Morale grade	D10 roll		VC/NLF			USMC
	ARVN	NVA	Main	Local	US	
Poor	1	–	–	1	–	–
Average	2–6	1–6	1–5	2–6	1–5	1–4
Fairly good	7–8	7–8	6–7	7–8	6–7	5–6
Good	9	9	8–9	9	8–9	7–8
Elite	10	10	10	10	10	9–10

Desertions were an additional problem that affected some ARVN units. However, these were not as widespread as some sources would have us believe and it certainly did not match up to the mass defection expected by the Communists. For most wargame purposes the desertions should be accounted for before the game begins. There is obviously no need to tell either side that there have been desertions – you can let them find out for themselves after the plans have been drawn up. Thus deserters can be as much a hindrance to the NVA/VC players as to the ARVN, as they are misidentified, spring ambushes and generally confuse the issue. A wargame rule might be that, once all the defending ARVN have been allocated their defensive positions, a die roll is made for each:

Table 3: ARVN desertion

Morale grade	Before action	At start of action	At 1st shot	Do not desert
Poor	1–2	3	4	5+
Average	–	1	2–3	4+
Good	–	1	2	3+
Elite	–	–	–	–

Die Roll Modifiers

Section NCO present	+1
M-16 armed unit	+1
Platoon sergeant present	+2
Platoon officer present	+2
Alone (night)	−2
Alone (day)	−1

In places, whole sub-units were reported as deserting (for example some elements of the 45th Infantry Regiment near Ban Me Thuot). Such mass desertions can be included in games, but balance must be considered as they would vary the weapons and strength of both sides. Just prior to the Tet Offensive, the first issue of M-16 assault rifles to the ARVN took place. This had a marked effect in improving effectiveness and morale in the ARVN units so equipped. Therefore an ARVN unit armed with M-16s should have a minimum morale grading of 'average'.

If the ARVN had problems, so too did the Communists; the desire for secrecy was confounded by their unreliable communications. The intended simultaneous offensive did not take place because the order was not received on time. Thus some units attacked at 0300 hours on 31 January as intended, others a day early, more a day late, still others even later. The effect of this would be to vary the alertness of the defenders. Timing should be the prerogative of the umpire or by means of a dicing system:

Table 4: NVA, VC/NLF assault timing

Type	30 Jan	31 Jan	1 Feb	2 Feb	3 Feb
NVA Regulars	1	2–9	10	–	–
NLF Main force	1–2	3–8	9	10	–
NLF Local force	1–3	4–6	7–8	9	10

Usually, ARVN units attacked on 30 January will be completely surprised; those on 31 Jan partially surprised; and those afterwards hardly surprised at all. The strength of the defenders should be increased as each day passes and soldiers return to duty.

Other disasters plagued the Communists. All communication was lost to the Saigon front shortly after the attacks started. VC/NLF units failed to maintain liaison in Saigon and other places, resulting in many objectives being attacked by too many units while others were attacked with inadequate strength. Units became lost in the cities after air and artillery strikes altered the geography.

The lack of good communications led to confusion, misdirection of reserves and slowed deployment. Any or all of these elements should be incorporated.

A prime factor in the failure to carry the objectives was the absence of a reserve force in support. Virtually every active service unit was allocated a primary objective. Thus units 'burned themselves out' through fatigue and casualties in ceaseless day and night operations. Then, inevitably, they lost the initiative and morale began to crack under the US and ARVN counter-attacks.

So far as we are concerned, this translates into the NLF/VC and NVA commanders not being allowed to receive reinforcements other than those they have allocated from their own commands. Fatigue rules are required for both sides, but are less of a burden to the US and ARVN players because of troops returning to duty or being flown in.

A further factor affecting the reduction of morale and performance of the NLF/VC and NVA was that the expected popular uprising against the Saigon Government failed to materialize. In fact, the local reaction seemed to range from apathy to hostility. Again the NLF and NVA soldiers had been briefed that the ARVN would crumble at the first attack. They did the opposite and put in a creditable performance in most cases. Thus NVA/VC/NLF morale should reduce the longer resistance lasts.

Some scenario suggestions might include:
1. NLF/VC sappers assault a USAF base to destroy aircraft on the ground. Points to consider: timing, strength of attackers and guard forces, terrain, field defences, breaching rules, surprise.
2. NLF/VC sappers attack a national radio station. Points to consider: as Scenario 1 plus morale of defenders.
3. NLF/VC suicide squad assault US Embassy. Points to consider: as Scenario 2.
4. Assaults on provincial, armed forces and government headquarters and other installations.

After the initial shock of the offensive, which was increased by an over-responsive media coverage, the US and ARVN launched a series of operations to recover lost ground. These were the long-awaited field battles the US generals had hoped for, the most famous and probably the most useful to the wargamer being the recapture of Hue by the ARVN and the US Marines. Street-fighting, search-and-destroy missions, patrols, water crossings and virtually every other type of military activity took place. Scenario options include:

1. Street-fighting and house-clearing with units of both sides in some confusion as to location and direction.

2. Relief of cut-off troops and evacuation of casualties under fire by US Marines or ARVN. It was Marine policy not only to evacuate the wounded but also to recover their dead for burial.

3. NVA or NLF/VC tank-stalking parties attempting to destroy enemy AFVs with satchel charges and/or rocket propelled grenades.

4. Clearing out a nest of snipers. This makes an excellent role-play scenario because it centres on the troops' willingness to take on the unknown.

These scenarios take place in relatively confined areas and at short ranges, leading to heavy casualties. Add a few booby-traps, minefields and civilian problems (refugees, civilians hiding in cellars, freed/escaped hostages, etc.) and the frustration of the war will come through.

Those desiring larger-scale actions should try some of the bigger operations staged in the follow up to the Tet Offensive:

1. NVA tank and infantry assault on, and capture of, Lang Vei Special Forces Camp (7 February).

2. Operation 'Quyet Thang' around Saigon to mop up and clear NVA/NLF forces from around the capital (11 March to 5 April).

3. Assaults on US fire bases; for example, at Kon Tum (26 March).

4. Operation 'Pegasus', the relief of Khe Sanh (1–14 April).

5. Operation 'Toan Thang', a major counter-offensive around Saigon (began 8 April).

6. Second and Third Battles for Saigon in May.

Air wargamers are not left out of this. Massive air strikes were launched against the besiegers of Khe Sanh, against targets inside North Vietnam and in support of the ground troops. Most scope for aerial combat lies in the Operation 'Rolling Thunder' raids against the North. Interesting scenarios could also be made from the many attempts at the rescue of shot-down aircrew. This would involve aircraft, helicopters, ground troops and good visibility and communications rules.

The selection of the rules for this period is a purely personal decision based on your own perspective of the war. For wargaming the Tet Offensive most of the modern period rules listed below are suitable, with some modifications for the peculiarities outlined above.

Commercial rules include the following.

Bodycount; Arclight Publications, 32 Milverton Road, Winchester.

Giac My; Platoon 20, Model Figures and Hobbies, Lower Balloo Road, Groomsport, County Down, BT19 2LU, Northern Ireland; and Ulster Imports Ltd, Box 1748, Champaign, Illinois 61820.

Hell by Daylight; Anschluss Publishing, 79 Godfrey Road, Spixworth, Norwich, Norfolk.

Firefight; Tabletop Games, 53 Mansefield Road, Daybrook, Nottingham, NG5 6BB.

Special Forces; MOD Games, 19 Chiltern Road, Sheffield, S6 4QX.

Skyfight (air combat); Tabletop Games, Skytrex, 28 Brook Street, Wymeswold, Loughborough, Leicestershire; and SG Simulations Inc., 1183 Cedar Street, Safety Harbor, Florida 34695.

Several magazines run articles periodically on the Vietnam War; these include: *Wargames Illustrated*, *Military Modelling* and *Wargames World*. These often give scenarios with special rules or information on how to amend existing rules. They are also useful sources of reviews and adverts for new products.

Board games include: *Sniper* by SPI; *Vietnam* by Victory Games; *Platoon* by Avalon Hill (the game of the film; the Director's royalties are paid into the Vietnam Veterans of America Foundation).